GIVE THEM
something better

America's Longest Living Culture
Shares their Family Secrets

Give Them Something Better: America's Longest Living Culture Shares their
Family Secrets
By Sarah Frain and Stephanie Howard
Cover design and layout by Sung Hoon Kang & Daniel Fachini
Food styling by Laura Goble
Photography by Kalman & Pabst Photo Group, www.kpphoto.com
Editing by Kimberley Stakal
ISBN for 8 ½ x 9 ¼: 978-0-615-45569-3
ISBN for 8 ½ x 11: 978-0-9835594-0-5
Library of Congress Control Number: 2011924086

Published by:
Sanare Life

Nutritional Information Disclaimer: The nutritional information for each recipe
was computed using Living Cookbook software. These analytical tools use
general averages for every ingredient and may not be 100% accurate or
completely reflective of the brands and ingredients you are using. The stats
provided are per serving and do not account for "optional" ingredients. The
comparison stats are provided by www.fatsecret.com and are typical of that
type of recipe.

Acknowledgements

We would like to show our appreciation to all of the people who helped us prepare this book. What began as a small fundraising cookbook became a lengthy learning process, and we're no less than thrilled with the beautiful book the project has turned into, which we hope will help people live longer and happier lives. Evelyn Kissinger, M.S., R.D. has been wonderful helping with research and writing, as well as encouraging us to do more than we think we can. Kristin Collins, also a Registered Dietitian, contributed to the Meal Planning section. Several real-life mothers tested our recipes in their own kitchens, including Monica Flower, Amie Hubbard, Sharon Pletcher, and Jan Smith, to name just a few. Thanks to the countless others who helped us with recipe editing and publishing—we couldn't have done it without you.

We owe an extra big "thank you" to our husbands and children, who pushed us to do something great with the talents God has given us. This encouragement helped us use valuable family time to achieve something that had been only a dream.

Most of all, we would like to thank the Master Designer for the wonderful way in which He provides so generously for our health and happiness.

"People talk about curing cancer and heart disease, and of course it is an important and worthy goal that can't happen soon enough. But there are simple things everyone could be doing right now that would save so much money and suffering – like drinking enough water every day, exercise, and eating healthy food. But everybody has his own idea about these things – it's their lives, after all. You can tell somebody what to do, but it's up to them whether they do it. But you can tell them how good you feel."

Ellsworh Wareham, MD, (see page 1)

Foreword

Parents who serve healthful meals at home do their children an enormous favor. In particular, children who are raised with a plant-based menu gain tremendous advantages. They have a strong measure of protection against the problems that so many people encounter-obesity, heart disease, diabetes, and even certain cancers. Studies also suggest that children raised on plant-based diets have higher IQs than their omnivorous classmates and, on average, will live years longer.

We can say this with confidence because we and many other research teams have put healthy diets to the test. In our studies, we have shown the power of healthful food choices to dramatically cut cholesterol levels, improve and even reverse diabetes, and restore overall good health. However, we were by no means the first to study the effects of good foods.

For decades, researchers have been studying Seventh-day Adventists. The reason is that, based on church teachings, Adventists are supposed to avoid alcohol, tobacco, caffeine, and meat. Nearly all Adventists are very good about the first three of those admonitions. But only about half of them follow vegetarian diets, while the other half include rather modest amounts of meat in their routines. This provides a natural experiment that has allowed researchers to test out the effects of including or excluding meat in the diet in a population that is otherwise generally health-conscious.

You now have in your hands a practical and engaging guide to preparing the very best foods in your own kitchen. You will be able to enjoy favorites like Vegetable Pot Pie, Lasagna, and Veggie Fajitas, and also learn some new tastes along the way. You'll get all the tips and menu planning support you need to help your family make the switch to a healthier diet and stick to it! All this and more is here in *Give them Something Better*.

By putting plant-foods at the center of your family's plate, your kids will thank you and so do I.

Neal Barnard, MD, President
Physicians Committee for Responsible Medicine

Table of Contents

LIVE LONG AND
prosper

Ellsworth Wareham lived in a beautiful home in the mountains of San Bernardino Valley. He was in need of an 8-foot-high wooden fence to border the steep edge of his sprawling property. A local contractor quoted Ellsworth a price of $5,000 to build the fence. After doing the math, Ellsworth realized he could buy the materials from a local hardware store and do it himself for just $2,000.

Many people in Ellsworth's situation would have hired the contractor. After all, he was more than 90 years old and money was not an issue. In the end, however, frugality won out and he built the fence himself. The following Tuesday, Ellsworth was at the hospital for open heart surgery, but he was not the patient. Ellsworth Wareham was the surgeon.

Dan Buettner, author of the National Geographic Study "Secrets of Longevity" and New York Times best-seller "Blue Zones," met Dr. Wareham while he was circling the globe in a quest to find the groups of people who lived the longest. Buettner found four groups of people whom he dubbed the "Blue Zones."

As you would expect, most of these people were found in secluded places. They were found in Okinawa, Japan, consuming soy foods on a regular basis. They were discovered in Sardinia, Italy, enjoying a Mediterranean diet. They were located in the pristine serenity of the Nicoya Peninsula in Costa Rica. However, Buettner found another Blue Zone in a highly unexpected place. The fourth Blue Zone was among the Seventh-day Adventists in California!

What makes Adventists unique? How do they live an average of 10 years longer than other Americans? Many organizations like the National Geographic and the American Cancer Society have asked that same question. Much research has been done to discover the answer. The Adventists are a great control group because they follow many similar lifestyle practices, such as not smoking or drinking alcohol, and many of them are vegetarian. They are a diverse group of people from every race, and color, growing by nearly a million members each year worldwide. By studying the Adventists, it has been determined that lifestyle choices contribute as much as 80 percent of one's health and longevity, while genetics only play a small part.

Dan Buettner condensed his findings into four major lifestyle choices that give the American Blue Zone their advantage: exercising regularly; eating a plant-based diet; taking a day off each week; and living with a purpose. As you turn through these pages you will find more information about helping your family live longer, healthier, happier lives and truly "Give them Something Better."

Buettner, Dan. The Blue Zones: Lessons for Living Longer from the People Who've Lived the Longest. National Geographic Society, 2008.

breakfast:

Don't leave home without it!

Breakfast is the most important meal of the day! But busy mornings often leave us with no choice but to skip breakfast or grab something quick on the way out the door. With proper planning, however, you can prepare a healthy, hearty breakfast in less time than it takes to go through a drive-thru. Check out the Now & Later tips that will show you how you can make many of these delicious options ahead of time and have them ready for a quick breakfast that is truly something better.

"(God) Who satisfieth thy mouth with good things; so that thy youth is renewed like the eagle's."

Psalm 103:5, KJV

menu

Light & Fluffy Pancakes

Peanut butter

Fruit Topping (page 7) or applesauce

Banana slices

Waffles

Peanut butter

Maple Topping (page 7) or applesauce

Fruit cup with almonds

Light and Fluffy Pancakes or Waffles

Many store-bought pancake and waffle mixes are full of additives and oxidized cholesterol, which stick to your arteries faster than anything. Making your own mix helps you to control what ingredients you use—and with a recipe this easy to prepare, your kids can even make you breakfast in bed!

DRY INGREDIENTS

1 ½ cups **whole wheat pastry flour**

½ cup unbleached white flour

½ cup cornmeal

1 tablespoon **aluminum-free baking powder**

½ teaspoon salt

WET INGREDIENTS:

1 ⅓ cups water

⅔ cup **nondairy milk**

¼ cup oil

1 tablespoon honey, **cane juice crystals**, or sugar

1 Mix dry ingredients together in a medium bowl.

2 Mix wet ingredients together in a separate small bowl.

3 Combine wet and dry ingredients together to form batter.

For Pancakes: Scoop batter with a ⅓ cup measuring cup for each pancake; pour onto a hot griddle and cook until golden brown on both sides, about 5 minutes.

For Waffles: Pour batter into a hot waffle iron and bake 6 to 7 minutes.

Makes 8 servings.

Make it a Mix on page 151 →

 NOW & LATER:

Waffles freeze well. Make an extra batch and put them in the freezer. Just pop them in the toaster to warm for a quick breakfast!

 CHANGE IT UP:

Try some of these add-ins: toasted nuts, peanut butter, pumpkin puree, grated apples, mashed or sliced bananas or berries.

Per 2 pancake serving	Cal	Fat	Sat. Fat	Chol	Sodium	Carbs	Fiber	Sugar	Protein
Traditional Recipe	260	8g	2g	0mg	612mg	43g	1g	13g	5g
Something Better	**214**	**8g**	**0g**	**0mg**	**133mg**	**32g**	**4g**	**3g**	**5g**

menu

Citrus French Toast

Fresh berries

Mixed nuts

Orange or grapefruit

Citrus French Toast

French toast is always a special treat for breakfast, but this French Toast, with a hint of orange, is amazing! The best part is that it doesn't have any eggs and it is sweetened naturally with dates. Not only is it a fancy treat, it is also good for you!

2 cups water, divided

½ cup **raw cashews**

¾ cup **whole wheat pastry flour**

½ cup dates

½ cup orange juice concentrate

1 tablespoon vanilla extract

¼ teaspoon **Cinnamon Substitute** (page 152) or ⅛ teaspoon ground coriander and ⅛ teaspoon cardamom

1 loaf whole grain bread

1 Blend cashews with 1 cup water until very smooth and creamy.

2 Add remaining ingredients to blender; blend until smooth. Pour into a flat, shallow dish.

3 Dip each slice of bread in batter and scrape off excess.

4 Place on a hot non-stick griddle and cook until golden brown on both sides.

Makes 8 servings.

NOW & LATER:

Make batter the night before and refrigerate for a quick breakfast in the morning. Save time by making an extra batch and freezing it for next time.

CHANGE IT UP:

You can change the flavor of the French Toast by trying different juice concentrates in place of the orange juice. Try white grape peach juice and serve with peach Fruit Sauce (page 7).

Per 2 piece serving	Cal	Fat	Sat. Fat	Chol	Sodium	Carbs	Fiber	Sugar	Protein
Traditional Recipe	260	12g	3g	180mg	640mg	40g	2g	8g	11g
Something Better	**249**	**5g**	**0g**	**0mg**	**223mg**	**41g**	**6g**	**12g**	**10g**

Maple Topping

Brilliant! We got this recipe from Jim and Neva Brackett's "Best Gourmet Recipes" available at www.seven-secrets.org. It has all the flavor of real maple syrup with half the sugar and calories! And guess what else? No high fructose corn syrup!

¼ cup water
1 ½ tablespoon cornstarch
1 cup maple syrup
1 cup water

1 Combine water and cornstarch in a small bowl; whisk until smooth and set aside.

2 Place syrup and water in a small saucepan; bring to a boil over high heat.

3 Slowly whisk in the dissolved cornstarch; remove from heat and serve.

Makes 16 servings.

Fruit Sauce

"This Fruit Sauce is naturally sweetened with real fruit juice and full of wonderful fruit to make your breakfast complete. Plus, if you happen to have leftovers, you can use them in several other recipes.

1 can 100% juice concentrate
(try apple, raspberry, or grape)
1 can water
⅓ cup cornstarch
¼ cup water
4 cups berries (blueberry, strawberry, blackberry, raspberry), or peaches, frozen or fresh

1 Combine juice concentrate and water in a medium saucepan; bring to a boil over medium-high heat.

2 Meanwhile, combine cornstarch and water together in a small bowl; whisk well and set aside.

3 Add cornstarch mixture to the boiling mixture, stirring constantly to avoid lumps and burning.

4 Cook about 1 minute, until the mixture is thick and liquid is clear.

5 Remove from heat; stir in berries.

Makes 12 servings.

 NOW & LATER:

Fruit Sauce can be used in a Granola Parfait (page 13) in place of the fresh fruit, in Fruit and Coconut Bars (page141) in place of the fruit jam, and is also delicious stirred into Hot Cereal (page 18).

NOW & LATER:

This keeps in the refrigerator for several days, so in a couple of days you can pull some of your homemade waffles out of the freezer for a special week day breakfast that is quick and easy.

Unsausages

I came across this recipe for sausages made out of oatmeal in Mary Bernt's book "Best of Veggies." You have got to try them—they are unbelievably good!

3 ½ cups water

¼ cup **Bragg's Liquid Aminos** or low sodium soy sauce

¼ cup **nutritional yeast flakes**

2 tablespoons oil

2 tablespoons onion powder

1 tablespoon maple syrup

1 tablespoon dried sage

1 tablespoon Italian seasoning

1 ½ teaspoon garlic powder

½ teaspoon cayenne pepper (optional)

3 ½ cups quick-cooking oats

1 Preheat oven to 350°F. Coat a baking sheet with non-stick cooking spray.

2 Combine all ingredients, except oats, in a medium saucepan; bring to a boil over high heat.

3 Remove from heat; add oats and stir well. Allow mixture to sit 5 minutes.

4 Scoop mixture into 2-inch round balls; place on prepared baking sheet and flatten gently with hands. Bake 15 minutes; flip sausages and bake an additional 10 minutes.

Makes 10 servings.

NOW & LATER:

Make a bunch of these for later. Make into patties and freeze on baking sheets. Once frozen, remove from pan and put in a freezer bag to store. To bake frozen patties, place on a baking sheet. Bake at 400°F for 20 to 25 minutes on each side.

TIP:

Vary amount of the cayenne pepper to change the spiciness.

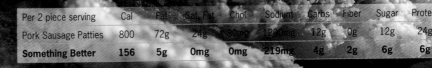

Per 2 piece serving	Cal	Fat	Sat. Fat	Chol	Sodium	Carbs	Fiber	Sugar	Protein
Pork Sausage Patties	800	72g	24g	80mg	1200mg	12g	0g	12g	24g
Something Better	**156**	**5g**	**0mg**	**0mg**	**219mg**	**4g**	**2g**	**6g**	**6g**

menu

Scrambled tofu

Oven Roasted Potatoes (page 120)

Whole grain English muffin with

non-hydrogenated margarine

Grapes

Orange juice

Breakfast Burrito

Scrambled Tofu

Oven Roasted Potatoes (page 120)

Whole grain tortilla

Salsa (page 32)

Aioli (page 130) or **soy sour cream**

Sliced green onions

Grapes

Scrambled Tofu

This is the recipe that changed my mind about tofu. I found it in Vicki Griffin's "Guilt-Free Gourmet" cookbook and it changed the way I look at tofu. I always thought tofu was mushy, but I found that the secret to good tofu is proper cooking…the longer you cook it, the firmer it becomes.

1 tablespoon oil

2 packages (14 ounces) water-packed **tofu**, extra firm, well drained

1 small onion, diced small (optional)

1 small green or bell pepper, diced small (optional)

¼ cup **nutritional yeast flakes**

3 tablespoons **Chicken Style Seasoning** (page 152) or commercial brand chicken seasoning

1 ½ teaspoons garlic powder

1 teaspoon onion powder

1 teaspoon salt

¼ teaspoon turmeric

parsley to garnish (optional)

1 Drain excess water from tofu. (See "How to" on page 150)

2 Heat oil in a large skillet over medium heat. Crumble tofu into pan with your fingers or use a spatula to break it up in the pan.

3 Add remaining ingredients to skillet; cook until tofu is browned and slightly dry, stirring occasionally. This could take from 10 to 30 minutes, depending on desired texture. The longer the tofu is cooked, the firmer the tofu will be.

Makes 6 servings.

Make it a Mix on page 151 →

 NOW & LATER:

Stir 1 to 2 cups into Nut Gravy (Page 12) or use in the Eggless Egg Salad (page 43) in place of the raw **tofu**. Or plan for leftovers and make Chilaquiles (page 72).

 CHANGE IT UP:

Add a few cups of diced cooked potatoes, or use up those leftover baked potatoes.

Per 1 cup serving	Cal	Fat	Sat. Fat	Chol	Sodium	Carbs	Fiber	Sugar	Protein
Scrambled Eggs (3)	300	26g	9g	600mg	316mg	3g	0g	2g	20g
Something Better	202	12g	2g	0mg	331mg	7g	4g	0g	20g

menu

Toast and gravy

Whole grain toast

Nut Gravy

Unsausages (page 8)

Fruit salad

Nut Gravy

Not growing up Adventist, I was raised on biscuits and sausage gravy. Not really a health food…until now! This great breakfast can satisfy the craving for a good country breakfast without all the fat and cholesterol—you can't beat that!

5 cups water, divided

1 ¼ cups Brazil nuts

6 tablespoons cornstarch

2 tablespoons onion powder

2 ½ tablespoons **nutritional yeast flakes**

1 ½ tablespoons **Braggs Liquid Aminos** or low sodium soy sauce

2 teaspoons **beef style seasoning**

1 teaspoon salt, to taste

ADD-INS

1 cup Scrambled Tofu (page 10) or vegetarian sausage crumbles (optional)

1 Place 2 ½ cups water and all remaining ingredients in blender.

2 Blend on high until very smooth and creamy, about 4 or 5 minutes; transfer to a medium saucepan.

3 Add remaining 2 ½ cups water to blender; blend briefly to clean out the blender. Transfer to saucepan with nut mixture.

4 Cook on medium heat until thick and creamy, stirring constantly to prevent burning.

5 Add optional Scrambled Tofu or sausage crumbles and stir.

Makes 18 servings.

 NOW & LATER:

Make a double batch of this gravy without the added **tofu** or sausage crumbles to serve over mashed potatoes. Also, try the gravy in Tater Tot Casserole (page 106).

TIP:

The selenium in Brazil nuts fights cancer and atherosclerosis. Eating this gravy is a great way to get your selenium and enjoy it too!

Per ⅓ cup serving	Cal	Fat	Sat. Fat	Chol	Sodium	Carbs	Fiber	Sugar	Protein
Sausage gravy	125	9g	3g	18mg	170mg	6g	0g	3g	6g
Something Better	**81**	**6g**	**1g**	**0mg**	**214mg**	**7g**	**4g**	**0g**	**2g**

menu

Breakfast Parfait

Granola

Fantastic Vanilla Pudding (page 145)

Fresh berries or Fruit Sauce (page 7)

Banana Slices

Whole grain toast with nut butter and jelly

Granola

Raisins or dates

Nondairy milk

Fresh berries or banana slices

½ grapefruit or orange

Granola

Dr. John Harvey Kellogg was a very famous Adventist doctor during the late 1800's who created granola and Kellogg's Cornflakes as a healthy breakfast for his patients who were trying his "new" vegetarian diet. So you can thank Adventists for the whole "cold cereal for breakfast" craze!

DRY INGREDIENTS

10 cups rolled or quick-cooking oats

3 cups rice cereal or

2 additional cups of oats

1 cup whole grain flour

1 ½ cups unsweetened coconut

1 ½ cups chopped nuts (walnuts, pecans, almonds or a combination)

WET INGREDIENTS

1 ½ cups water

1 to 1 ¼ cups brown sugar

½ cup oil

2 tablespoons vanilla extract

1 ½ teaspoons salt

1 Preheat oven to 200°F.

2 Mix dry ingredients together in a large bowl.

3 Mix wet ingredients together in a separate small bowl.

4 Add wet mixture to dry mixture. Mix gently with a spoon or your hands until all of the ingredients are moistened.

5 Spread onto two large baking sheets.

6 Bake overnight (6 to 8 hours) or bake at 300°F for 2 hours, stirring every 15 minutes.

7 Cool completely before storing in an airtight container.

Makes 40 servings.

 TIP:

Turn off the oven and leave granola in the oven until it has cooled. This makes the granola extra crunchy!

TIP:

If you like chunks in your granola, gently squeeze little handfuls of the mixture as you put it on the baking sheets.

 NOW & LATER:

Use in Breakfast Parfaits (page 13), Banana Muffins (page 21), or Easy Pie Crust (page 143).

Per ½ cup serving	Cal	Fat	Sat. Fat	Chol	Sodium	Carbs	Fiber	Sugar	Protein
Traditional Recipe	300	15g	3g	0mg	14mg	32g	5g	12g	9g
Something Better	**177**	**8g**	**1g**	**0mg**	**93mg**	**24g**	**3g**	**6g**	**4g**

menu

Peach and Blueberry Crisp

Mixed nuts

Fresh fruit

Peach and Blueberry Crisp

Crisp is usually a dessert food, but if you make it right, full of whole grains and yummy fruit, you can eat it for breakfast. How great is that!

FILLING

1 can (12 ounces) 100% white grape-peach juice concentrate

½ cup water

8 cups peaches, peeled and sliced (fresh, frozen, or canned)

2 cups blueberries (fresh or frozen)

1 Preheat oven to 350°F.

2 Pour juice concentrate into a large saucepan and cook over medium heat until boiling.

3 Mix cornstarch with water in a small bowl. Add to the boiling juice and cook until thickened, stirring constantly.

4 Add peaches and stir well to mix. (If you are using frozen peaches or your peaches are not quite ripe and need to soften more, add them in Step 1 and bring them to a boil with the juice.

5 Pour peach mixture into a 9-by-13-inch baking pan; top with blueberries.

CRISP TOPPING

1 ½ **whole wheat pastry flour**

1 ½ cups quick-cooking oats

½ cup ground **flax seeds** or wheat germ

⅔ unsweetened coconut

½ teaspoon salt

½ cup oil

1 Mix all ingredients, except oil, together in a medium bowl.

2 Drizzle oil over ingredients and mix well.

3 Spread crisp topping evenly over fruit. Bake 45 minutes, until topping is golden and juices bubble.

Makes 16 servings.

 NOW & LATER:

Make it ahead! After fruit crisp is assembled, cover with tin foil and refrigerate. Bake in the morning for a delicious hot breakfast!

 CHANGE IT UP:

This fruit crisp is great. It works with almost any kind of fruit that you have. Try this combination or get creative.

Per ½ cup serving	Cal	Fat	Sat. Fat	Chol	Sodium	Carbs	Fiber	Sugar	Protein
Traditional Recipe	300	15g	3g	0mg	14mg	32g	5g	12g	9g
Something Better	**177**	**8g**	**1g**	**0mg**	**93mg**	**24g**	**3g**	**6g**	**4g**

Oatmeal Doesn't Have to be Boring!

So you say you don't like oatmeal...have you ever had it like this?

1 Brown sugar and raisins

2 Honey and granola (page 14)

3 Mashed banana and applesauce

4 Granola (page 14) and **nondairy milk**

5 Raspberry **soy yogurt** and dried cranberries

6 Apricot fruit spread, dried apricots, and sliced almonds

7 Sliced strawberries and strawberry **soy yogurt**

8 Maple syrup and chopped toasted pecans

9 Canned crushed pineapple, sliced bananas, and chopped macadamia nuts

10 Sliced bananas, vanilla **soy yogurt**, and granola (page 14) or nuts

11 **Natural peanut butter** and strawberry fruit spread

12 Chopped dates and walnuts

13 Coarsely chopped canned peaches and **soy creamer**

14 Diced dried apricots or diced dried mixed fruit and honey

15 Apple or pumpkin butter and walnuts

16 Blueberry fruit spread and vanilla **soy yogurt**

17 Orange marmalade and dried cranberries

18 Coarsely chopped apples, brown sugar, and dates

19 Orange marmalade and orange segments with **nondairy milk**

20 Cherry all-fruit jam, toasted sliced almonds, and wheat germ

21 Barley sweetened **carob chips**, chopped pecans, and coconut

22 Berries sprinkled with a little sugar and **Cinnamon Substitute** (page 152)

23 Sliced bananas and **carob chips**

24 Leftover Fruit Sauce (page 7) and **nondairy milk**

25 **Natural peanut butter** and maple syrup or honey

> *Hot cereal is a great way to start the day, especially in the winter. Quick oats are a good option but it is fun to change things up a bit and try other whole grain cereals. So here is a no fuss way to cook other whole grains and have them waiting for you in the morning!*

Crock Pot Oatmeal

TIP:

Try other whole grains like rice, barley, millet, etc. or mix several grains together. Otherwise, you can use a pre-mixed 7-grain cereal.

1 ¼ cups water

½ cup 7-grain cereal

⅛ teaspoon salt

1 Spray crock pot with non-stick cooking spray.

2 Add all ingredients to the crock pot.

3 Cook on high overnight

Apple Pecan Muffins

Who can resist the sweet taste of apples and toasted pecans? The good news is that you don't have to. These wonderful muffins are low in fat and full of whole grains and fiber. So you can have your muffin and eat it, too!

TOPPING

¼ cup toasted pecans, chopped

2 tablespoons brown sugar

¼ teaspoon cardamom

⅛ teaspoon coriander (optional) or

½ teaspoon **Cinnamon Substitute** (page 152)

DRY INGREDIENTS

2 ¼ cup **whole wheat pastry flour** or a combination of **whole wheat pastry flour** and unbleached white flour

1 tablespoon cornstarch

2 teaspoons **aluminum-free baking powder**

½ teaspoon salt

WET INGREDIENTS

1 cup unsweetened applesauce

¾ cup **nondairy milk**

½ cup **sucanat** or brown sugar

¼ cup oil

1 tablespoon ground **flax seeds**

1 teaspoon vanilla extract

1 medium apple, diced

1 Preheat oven to 400°F.

2 Coat muffin tins with non-stick cooking spray or line with muffin liners. Mix topping ingredients together in a small bowl.

3 Mix dry ingredients together in a medium bowl.

4 Mix wet ingredients together, except diced apples, in a separate medium bowl.

5 Add dry ingredients to wet ingredients in two batches, mixing until just combined. Fold in diced apples.

6 Fill each muffin cup ¾ full; top with 1 ½ teaspoons of the topping.

7 Bake 20 minutes, or until a toothpick inserted in the middle comes out clean.

8 When cool enough to handle, transfer to wire racks to cool completely.

Makes 15 muffins.

Per 1 muffin serving	Cal	Fat	Sat. Fat	Chol	Sodium	Carbs	Fiber	Sugar	Protein
Traditional Recipe	450	12g	3g	60mg	340mg	80g	2g	49g	7g
Something Better	**174**	**6g**	**0g**	**0mg**	**71mg**	**29g**	**4g**	**13g**	**3g**

Lemon Poppy Seed Muffins

My kids love lemon, lemon anything really, but when you put lemon in a muffin…you've really got something!

DRY INGREDIENTS

2 cups and **2** tablespoons white **whole wheat pastry flour**

½ cup **cane juice crystals** or sugar

1 ½ tablespoons poppy seeds

1 tablespoon **aluminum-free baking powder**

½ teaspoon salt

WET INGREDIENTS

¾ cup **nondairy milk**

⅓ cup oil

¼ cup fresh lemon juice

2 tablespoons lemon zest

2 teaspoons vanilla extract

GLAZE (OPTIONAL)

⅔ cup powdered sugar

1 tablespoon fresh lemon juice

1 Preheat oven to 375°F.

2 Coat muffin tins with non-stick cooking spray or line with muffin liners. Mix dry ingredients together in a large bowl.

3 Make a well in the center of dry ingredients; add wet ingredients. Mix until combined but do not over mix.

4 Fill each muffin cup ¾ full; and bake 23 to 27 minutes, until a toothpick inserted in the middle comes out clean.

5 When cool enough to handle, transfer to wire racks to cool completely.

GLAZE

1 Mix powdered sugar and lemon juice together in a small bowl.

2 Dip the top of each cooled muffin in glaze.

3 Store in an airtight container for 2 to 3 days.

Makes 10 muffins.

Per 1 muffin serving	Cal	Fat	Sat. Fat	Chol.	Sodium	Carbs	Fiber	Sugar	Protein
Traditional Recipe	470	20g	5g	90mg	660mg	68g	2g	40g	7g
Something Better	**174**	**7g**	**0g**	**0mg**	**88mg**	**25g**	**3g**	**9g**	**4g**

Banana Muffins

Gorgeous! These muffins are a work of art—and they taste as good as they look.

WET INGREDIENTS

⅓ cup hot water

2 tablespoons ground **flax seeds**

2 cups mashed banana (about 3 large)

⅔ cup **nondairy milk**

¾ cup **sucanat** or brown sugar

⅓ cup oil

2 teaspoons vanilla extract

DRY INGREDIENTS

4 cups **whole wheat pastry flour**

½ cup walnuts or pecans, chopped

4 teaspoons **aluminum-free baking powder**

1 teaspoon salt

TOPPING

½ cup dried banana chips, crushed (optional)

1 Preheat oven to 400°F. Coat muffin tins with non-stick cooking spray or line with cupcake liners.

2 Mix flax seeds and hot water together in a small bowl. Set aside.

3 Combine remaining wet ingredients in a medium bowl; add reserved flax mixture and mix well. Mix dry ingredients together in a separate medium bowl.

4 Mix wet ingredients into dry ingredients. (The batter will be thick.)

5 Fill each muffin cup ¾ full; top with banana chips.

6 Bake 15 to 18 minutes, until a toothpick inserted in the middle comes out clean. Makes 18 muffins.

 CHANGE IT UP:

Banana Crunch Muffins: Add 1 cup of Granola (page 14) to the batter.

Per 1 muffin serving	Cal	Fat	Sat Fat	Chol	Sodium	Carbs	Fiber	Sugar	Protein
Traditional Recipe	470	18g	3g	40mg	380mg	70g	2g	43g	7g
Something Better	**228**	**8g**	**2g**	**0mg**	**112mg**	**37g**	**5g**	**13g**	**5g**

Pineapple Muffins

Check it out—a fat free muffin! It's almost too good to be true...but it's not! You need to taste it to believe it!

WET INGREDIENTS

1 can (**20** ounces crushed pineapple, packed in pineapple juice, undrained

⅔ cup unsweetened applesauce

¼ cup water

2 tablespoons lemon juice

1 tablespoon **flax seeds**

DRY INGREDIENTS

2 cups oat flour

2 cups **whole wheat pastry flour**

⅔ cup **cane juice crystals** or sugar

2 tablespoons **aluminum-free baking powder**

1 teaspoon salt

TOPPING

¼ cup raw sugar

1 Preheat oven to 350°F. Coat muffin tins with non-stick cooking spray or line with cupcake liners.

2 Mix flax seeds and hot water together in a small bowl. Set aside.

3 Mix dry ingredients together in a large bowl.

4 Add wet ingredients, including reserved flax seed mixture; stir until combined, but don't over mix. (The batter will be thick.)

5 Fill each muffin cup ¾ full and sprinkle with sugar.

6 Bake 20 to 30 minutes, until a toothpick inserted in the middle comes out clean.

7 Allow to cool at least 15 minutes before serving.

Makes 18 muffins.

 TIP:

Try other whole grains like rice, barley, millet, etc. or mix several grains together. Otherwise, you can use a pre-mixed 7- grain cereal.

TIP:

The flax and water mixture replaces eggs in the original recipe. Check out page 153 to find out how to use it in your recipes.

Per 1 muffin serving	Cal	Fat	Sat. Fat	Chol	Sodium	Carbs	Fiber	Sugar	Protein
Traditional Recipe	470	17g	4g	90mg	640mg	75g	2g	43g	7g
Something Better	**156**	**0g**	**0g**	**0mg**	**107mg**	**35g**	**3g**	**15g**	**4g**

GET
moving!

Imagine how your life will be in 30, 40, or even 50 years. Your kids are all grown up and the hustle-bustle days of parenthood are over. How are you going to live your life? If you make the right choices now, your future might look something like this...

Just imagine... You have a play date with your grandkids—a day at the park filled with swinging and sliding. You and your husband are planning your dream trip to Hawaii. You look forward to long walks on the beach, biking around the island and an exhilarating paraglide excursion. Every day is an adventure, and you have the health and energy you need to enjoy it.

When Dan Buettner discovered the Blue Zones, he found people doing all of these things and more—and they were doing them well into their 90's! His research has proven that the choices you make now have a significant impact on your quality of life in the future. We all make choices each and every day, and those choices impact our health, our lifestyle, and our longevity.

People in the Blue Zones stay active. While they may go to the gym, that was not key to their success. The key is daily activity. Those in America's Blue Zone don't fight for the closest parking spots. They park further away and enjoy the walk. They use the stairs instead of the elevator. They play ball outside instead of watching the game on TV. In short, Adventists who live longer get moving every day.

Being active is one of the keys to health and longevity, bringing almost immediate results. In the short term, it can produce such benefits as reducing stress, boosting brain power, and improving your mood. At the same time, an active lifestyle can also protect in the long run against high blood pressure, heart disease, and diabetes—cutting your risk right in half. Living the Adventist lifestyle doesn't guarantee you will live to be 100 or never get sick, but the studies do show that the choice to be active now definitely affects your quality of life—both now and in the future.

Why don't you get moving today and give your family "something better" in the future?

salads &
dressings

Eat the rainbow

There is a saying that goes like this: "Strive for 5, but 8 is great!" That is, try to eat five to eight servings of fruits and vegetables a day. Don't worry, that's not as much food as you're probably thinking! A serving of fresh fruit or vegetable is usually as little as a ½ cup, and that's easy to sneak into your diet with a quick and delicious salad. Salads are a great way to eat the rainbow—a few slices of something green, a few cubes of something orange, a sliver of something red, and you've just created a nutritious work of art!

"Beloved, I pray that in all respects you may prosper and be in good health, just as your soul prospers."

3 John 1:2, NASB

Favorite Salad Combos

Creating your own salads is fun and easy here are a few salad combos to get you started.

Greek Salad
Red Romaine

Romaine

Radicchio

Artichoke hearts

Red onions

Tomatoes

Chickpeas

Pine nuts

Fake Feta (page 129)

Garlic Feta Dressing

(page 33)

Spinach Salad
Spinach

Cucumbers

Red peppers

Olives

Tomatoes

Toasted walnuts

Nondairy parmesan

Baco Bits

Poppy seed dressing

Italian Salad
Romaine

Spring mix

Basil

Tomatoes

Red onions

Cucumbers

Olives

Nondairy parmesan

Favorite Italian

Dressing (page 34)

Santa Fe Salad
Romaine

Iceberg

Cilantro

Corn

Tomatoes

Avocados

Kidney beans

Taco Ranch Dressing

(page 34)

Salads & Dressings

Cobb Salad

Iceberg lettuce

Romaine

Parsley

Tomatoes

Mushrooms

Hard Boiled "Eggs"

(page 34)

Ranch Dressing (page 34)

Soy turkey or ham slices

Baco Bits

Asian Salad

Romaine

Cabbage

Cilantro

Scallions

Cucumbers

Carrots

Edamame

Chow mein noodles

Toasted sesame seeds

Cabbage Salad Dressing

(page 31)

All American Salad

Bibb

Boston

Iceberg

Carrots

Red onions

Radishes

Red peppers

Tomatoes

Soy cheddar

Baco Bits

Ranch Dressing

(page 34)

Broccoli Salad

Don't be shocked, but there is no lettuce in this salad. Sounds crazy, I know…but I think you'll like it.

SALAD

1 large bunch broccoli, washed and cut into bite-size pieces

½ cup red onion, finely chopped

½ cup raisins

½ cup sunflower seeds

½ cup imitation bacon bits (such as Baco Bits) or

6 pieces vegetarian breakfast strips, cooked and crumbled (optional)

DRESSING

1 cup Aioli (page 130) or commercial **soy mayonnaise**

2 tablespoons lemon juice

2 tablespoons **cane juice crystals** or sugar

1 Combine the salad ingredients in a large bowl and set aside.

2 Combine the dressing ingredients in a small bowl.

3 Pour dressing over salad and toss gently. Serve immediately.

Makes 12 servings.

CHANGE IT UP:

This salad is very flexible and can be changed according to your preferences. You can use a combination of broccoli and cauliflower in the salad. Switch dried cranberries for the raisins or peanuts for the sunflower seeds… the possibilities are endless!

TIP:

The elements of the salad can be made ahead then combined right before serving.

*A lot of this fat and sugar comes from the "good for you" fats in the sunflower seeds and sugars in naturally sweet raisins.

Per ½ cup serving	Cal	Fat	Sat. Fat	Chol	Sodium	Carbs	Fiber	Sugar	Protein
Something Better	199	15g*	0g	0mg	127mg	12g	2g	7g	3g

Coleslaw

Cabbage is packed with phytochemicals and antioxidants, so eat it as often as you can. Coleslaw is a delicious way to get all of the benefits of cabbage. My favorite way to eat this slaw is inside my BBQ Chicken Sandwich (page 96). The sweet, creamy, and crunchy combination is great with the tangy spice of BBQ!

4 cups cabbage, shredded
¼ cup carrot, grated
⅓ cup Aioli (page 130) or commercial **soy mayonnaise**
2 tablespoons lemon juice
2 tablespoons green onion, finely minced
1 tablespoon **cane juice crystals** or sugar
¼ teaspoon salt (or to taste)

1 Combine cabbage and carrots in a large bowl.
2 Mix together remaining ingredients in a medium bowl.
3 Pour over cabbage mixture and mix well.
4 Refrigerate 2 to 4 hours and serve.
  Makes 12 servings.

TIP:

This is a great place to use your food processor! Use it to shred your cabbage and carrots.

SHORTCUT:

A bag of pre-cut slaw mix makes this recipe extra quick and easy to put together.

Per ⅓ cup serving	Cal	Fat	Sat. Fat	Chol	Sodium	Carbs	Fiber	Sugar	Protein
Traditional Recipe	90	8g	1g	4mg	174mg	5g	1g	3g	1g
Something Better	**54**	**4g**	**0g**	**0mg**	**94mg**	**3g**	**0g**	**2g**	**0g**

Mom's Potato Salad

We call this Mom's potato salad because I was trying to copy my mother-in-law's recipe while also making it a little healthier. Don't tell her, but I think mine is better, and it is cholesterol-free!

SALAD

6 cups red skinned potatoes, diced

1 ½ cups celery, finely chopped

½ onion, finely chopped

DRESSING

½ to ¾ cup **pickle relish**

1 to 2 tablespoons **Chicken Style Seasoning** (page 152) or commercial brand chicken seasoning

1 teaspoon salt

½ to 1 cup Aioli (page 130) or commercial **soy mayonnaise**

1 Boil potatoes in a large pot of water until tender. Drain and let cool. Transfer to a large bowl.

2 Add celery and onions to potatoes. Set aside

3 Mix dressing ingredients in a small bowl.

4 Pour dressing over salad ingredients; mix well. Chill 2 to 4 hours and serve.

Makes 16 servings.

 TIP:

We love using **pickle relish** made with lemon juice instead of vinegar. The flavor is wonderful and it is more healthful.

Per ½ cup serving	Cal	Fat	Sat. Fat	Chol	Sodium	Carbs	Fiber	Sugar	Protein
Traditional Recipe	200	11g	2g	95mg	739	16g	2g	0g	3g
Something Better	**103**	**5g**	**0g**	**0mg**	**233mg**	**13g**	**1g**	**3g**	**1g**

7 Layer Salad

A blast from the past! Seven-layer salads were very popular a few years ago, but we are not the type to throw out a good recipe just because everybody else moves on to the next fad! This salad is quick and easy to put together, and you can use any vegetables you like. Besides, the presentation in stunning when made in a glass bowl.

SALAD

8 cups mixed greens, torn into bite-sized pieces

3 carrots, grated

1 cup frozen peas, thawed

2 tomatoes, sliced

1 cucumber, sliced

1 bell pepper, diced (red, yellow, or orange)

DRESSING

2 cups Aioli (Page 130) or commercial **soy mayonnaise**

½ cup lemon juice

¼ cup **cane juice crystals** or sugar

FINISH IT OFF

4 green onions, chopped

1 Layer salad ingredients in a large clear glass bowl.

2 Mix dressing ingredients in a medium bowl; pour over salad.

3 Top with green onions.

Makes 32 servings.

 TIP:

This salad is great to make a day ahead of time. Just leave the dressing off and put it on up to 4 hours before serving.

Per ⅓ cup serving	Cal	Fat	Sat. Fat	Chol	Sodium	Carbs	Fiber	Sugar	Protein
Traditional Recipe	90	8g	1g	4mg	174mg	5g	1g	3g	1g
Something Better	**177**	**8g**	**1g**	**0mg**	**93mg**	**24g**	**3g**	**6g**	**4g**

Chinese Cabbage Salad

Everybody LOVES this salad! It is easy to throw together and full of cabbage, which is so good for you!

CRUNCHY TOPPING

1 tablespoon oil

1 package (3 ounces) Ramen noodles, broken into small pieces (discard seasoning packet)

½ cup sliced almonds

2 tablespoons sesame seeds

DRESSING

⅓ cup oil

⅓ cup **cane juice crystals** or sugar

2 tablespoons lemon juice

2 teaspoons **Bragg's Liquid Aminos** or low sodium soy sauce

SALAD

1 large head cabbage, shredded

⅓ cup carrot, shredded

5 to 6 scallions, chopped

1 Heat oil in a medium skillet over medium. Add Ramen noodles and almonds; cook until golden brown, about 5 minutes, stirring occasionally. Add sesame seeds; cook 1 minute, stirring. Cool completely.

2 Pour dressing ingredients into a container with a tight fitting lid. Shake well; set aside.

3 Combine cabbage and scallions in a large bowl.

4 Add crunchy topping and dressing to the salad just before serving; mix well.

Makes 16 servings.

 TIP:

Those little sesame seeds cook fast—make sure you watch them closely.

 TIP:

Try adding other shredded vegetables in with the cabbage. Carrots, broccoli, and red cabbage add some real color to this delicious salad.

Per ⅓ cup serving	Cal	Fat	Sat. Fat	Chol	Sodium	Carbs	Fiber	Sugar	Protein
Something Better	116	8g	1g	0mg	88mg	9g	1g	4g	2g

Salsa

I think my brother-in-law eats salsa at every meal! This great homemade version is best when you can get fresh garden tomatoes—but it is still great even if you use canned tomatoes.

3 medium tomatoes, diced small
½ large onion, diced finely
2 cloves garlic, minced
1 can (15 ounces) diced tomatoes
1 bunch green onions, diced (optional)
1 can (4 ounces) green chilies or one fresh jalapeno, minced
2 tablespoons lime or lemon juice
2 tablespoons fresh cilantro, chopped
½ to ¾ teaspoon salt

1 Mix all ingredients in a small bowl until everything is evenly distributed.
Makes 12 servings.

TIP:

To save time, use your food processor to chop and mix everything, but make sure you just pulse it or you may end up with tomato sauce instead!

TIP:

Use a 28-ounce can of petite diced tomatoes in place of the 3 fresh tomatoes.

Cucumber, Tomato and Avocado Salad

There isn't much to this salad, but you will be amazed at how much you like it. Sometimes simple is best. It goes great with Dominican Beans (page 84) or anything or Chilaquiles (page 72).

1 medium cucumber
1 large tomato
1 medium avocado
1 tablespoon lemon juice (fresh is best!)
¼ teaspoon salt

1 Dice vegetables; combine in a large bowl.
2 Add lemon juice and salt to vegetables; toss well. Serve immediately.

TIP:

Amounts may vary depending on the size of your vegetables. You want equal amounts of each vegetable.

Thousand Island Dressing

½ cup commercial **soy mayonnaise**

2 tablespoons Ketchup (page 130)

1 tablespoon lemon juice

2 teaspoons **cane juice crystals** or sugar

2 teaspoons sweet **pickle relish**

1 teaspoon finely minced white onion

⅛ teaspoon salt

1 Mix all ingredients together in a medium bowl. Chill.
   Makes 12 servings.

Per 1 tablespoon serving	Cal	Fat	Sat. Fat	Chol	Sodium	Carbs	Fiber	Sugar	Protein
Traditional Recipe	59	6g	1g	4mg	138mg	2g	0g	2g	0g
Something Better	**30**	**2g**	**0g**	**4mg**	**77mg**	**3g**	**0g**	**2g**	**0g**

Garlic Feta Dressing

¾ cup Fake Feta (page 129)

½ cup commercial **soy sour cream** or Aioli (page 130)

½ cup commercial **soy mayonnaise**

2 tablespoons liquid from Fake Feta (page 129)

1 tablespoon fresh basil, minced or ½ teaspoon dried basil

1 teaspoon **cane juice crystals** or sugar

¼ teaspoon salt

1 clove garlic, minced

nondairy milk, unsweetened, as needed to reach desired consistency

1 Mix all ingredients together, adding nondairy milk as need to reach desired consistency.
2 Chill at least 2 hours to allow flavors to blend together.
   Makes 12 servings.

Per 2 tablespoon serving	Cal	Fat	Sat. Fat	Chol	Sodium	Carbs	Fiber	Sugar	Protein
Something Better	**53**	**4g**	**1g**	**0mg**	**142mg**	**5g**	**0g**	**2g**	**0g**

Hard Boiled "Eggs"

2 cups water
1 package (14 ounces) extra-firm **tofu**, water-packed, cubed or crumbled
2 tablespoons **Chicken Style Seasoning** (page 152) or commercial brand chicken seasoning

1 Combine all ingredients in a medium saucepan; bring to a boil over high heat.
2 Simmer 20 minutes; drain off excess liquid.
   Serve in Mom's Potato Salad (page 29) or on Cobb Salad (page 26).
   Makes 16 servings.

Per 2 tablespoon serving	Cal	Fat	Sat. Fat	Chol	Sodium	Carbs	Fiber	Sugar	Protein
Hard Boiled Egg	77	5g	2g	211mg	139mg	1g	0g	1g	6g
Something Better	**29**	**2g**	**0g**	**0mg**	**4mg**	**0g**	**0g**	**7g**	**3g**

Favorite Italian Dressing

⅔ cup oil
¼ cup lemon juice
2 tablespoons water
1 packet (7 ounces) Italian dressing mix

1 Mix all ingredients together in a small bowl. Chill before serving.
   Makes 16 servings.

Per ⅓ cup serving	Cal	Fat	Sat. Fat	Chol	Sodium	Carbs	Fiber	Sugar	Protein
Something Better	**81**	**9g**	**1g**	**0mg**	**486mg**	**0g**	**0g**	**1g**	**0g**

Ranch Dressing

1 cup commercial **soy mayonnaise**
¼ cup **nondairy milk**, unsweetened, as needed to desired consistency
2 tablespoons Saucy Ranch Seasoning (available from The **Vegetarian Express**), or any dairy-free, MSG-free Ranch dressing packet mix)

1 Whisk all ingredients together in a small bowl until smooth.
2 Chill to allow flavors to blend.
   Makes about 10 servings

CHANGE IT UP:

Taco Ranch Dressing: Add Taco Seasoning (page 151) to taste.

Per ⅓ cup serving	Cal	Fat	Sat. Fat	Chol	Sodium	Carbs	Fiber	Sugar	Protein
Something Better	**92**	**8g**	**1g**	**0mg**	**96mg**	**0g**	**0g**	**0g**	**0g**

EATING TO
live

Oprah has tried it. Dr. Oz has recommended it. Even Bill Clinton and Mike Tyson do it. It seems like more and more people are trying a plant-based diet, and with good reason. What was once thought to be a diet for only the fringe of society has become well-respected by today's top athletes, celebrities, and business professionals who use it to gain a competitive edge. Studies show that a plant-based diet improves health and brain function, prevents or controls heart disease, reduces cancer risks, and can also control or even reverse type 2 diabetes—not to mention the many ways it helps the environment.

All of the people living in the Blue Zones follow a largely plant-based diet. The Seventh-day Adventists, who make up America's Blue Zone, have been advocating the plant-based diet for more than one-hundred years—long before it was the popular thing to do! Because of this, more than 300 studies have been done on the Adventists' lifestyle, and the research has shown that this diet provides them with a significant edge in health and longevity, adding as much as a decade to one's life.

One such study compared the health differences between vegetarian Adventists and meat-eating Adventists. The vegetarian Adventists were leaner and healthier. The Adventists who ate meat just four times a week experienced a four-fold increase in risk of a fatal heart attack, a 65% increase in colon or ovarian cancer, and twice the risk of bladder cancer. When meat was eaten every day, the risk of developing diabetes and dementia doubled.

Fortunately, benefiting from a plant-based diet doesn't have to be complicated. We designed this book to make it easy to implement a plant-based diet in your family. In order to keep your family happy making these changes, you need to start slowly. Try one or two new recipes a week, and as you find recipes your family enjoys, you can add them into your monthly meal plan. Before long you will find yourself preparing an array of plant-based foods that your family loves!

Start to build a healthy foundation for your family so that together you can all enjoy "something better."

Fraser, Gary E. Diet, Life Expectancy, and Chronic Disease: Studies of Seventh-day Adventists and Other Vegetarians. Oxford University Press, 2003

main meals

Your family favorites made better

Variety is the spice of life. We have provided you with an abundance of delicious recipes – so many, in fact, that you are sure to find something for everyone. There are seven meal categories with five recipes in each one in order to provide you with five weeks of menu planning options. Read "What's for Dinner" on page 157 to learn how to use these categories to create a healthy meal plan your family will love.

"That thy way may be known upon earth, thy saving health among all nations."

Psalm 67:2, KJV

menu

Corn Chowder

Melty Muffins

Broccoli & carrots

with Ranch Dressing (page 34)

Per 1 cup serving	Cal	Fat	Sat. Fat	Chol	Sodium	Carbs	Fiber	Sugar	Protein
Traditional Recipe	220	10g	2g	14mg	796mg	28g	3g		6g
Something Better	**190**	**3g**	**0g**	**0mg**	**230mg**	**40g**	**4g**	**3g**	**7g**

Corn Chowder

When the craving strikes for something rich and comforting, this hearty chowder hits the spot! It's a dairy-free version of the classic corn chowder, made with less fat and calories than the traditional recipe; I bet you'll even like this one better.

7 cups potatoes, peeled and diced

1 medium onion, chopped

½ cup **raw cashews**

3 cans (15 ounces) corn, divided

¼ cup **Chicken Style Seasoning** (page 152) or commercial brand chicken seasoning

¼ cup **nutritional yeast flakes**

1 teaspoon dried basil

1 teaspoon onion powder

1 Place potatoes and onions in a large pot and cover with water; bring to a boil over high heat. Reduce to a low boil; cook until potatoes are tender.

2 Place 2 cups of the potato and onion mixture in a blender; add cashews and half of one can of corn. Blend until smooth, adding additional water as necessary.

3 Pour contents of blender, along with the remaining ingredients, into pan with cooked potatoes and simmer until heated through. Add water as needed to reach desired consistency.

Makes 12 servings.

TIP:
Do not boil; the soup will curdle.

Melty Muffins

When friends stop by for a visit, throw together some Melty Muffins in a jiffy. They remind us of mini pizzas and everybody loves them! The Melty Cheeze is made from cashews, which adds protein and healthy fat to this simple meal your family will ask for again and again.

2 cups Melty Cheeze (page 127)

1 cup onion, diced

¾ cup black or green olives, chopped

1 can (4 ounces) mild green chilies, chopped

¼ cup pimentos or fresh red pepper, chopped

12 whole grain English muffins, split

1 Preheat oven to 400°F.

2 Pour Melty Cheeze into a medium bowl. Add onions, olives, chilies, and pimentos; stir well.

3 Place English muffins on a large baking sheet; spread about 2 tablespoons of the cheese mixture onto each muffin.

4 Bake 10 minutes, or until cheese is bubbly and muffins are crispy around the edges.

Makes 8 servings.

Per 3 muffin serving	Cal	Fat	Sat. Fat	Chol	Sodium	Carbs	Fiber	Sugar	Protein
Something Better	292	6g	1g	0mg	95mg	51g	9g	10g	13g

menu

Minestrone

It doesn't get any easier than this, and the whole family loves it! This soup is full of fiber and protein from the beans. Even my son, who is a little "anti-soup," asks for it.

4 cups vegetable broth

2 cans (15 ounces) beans, rinsed and drained (kidney, great northern, garbanzo, etc.)

2 cups frozen mixed vegetables

1 medium onion, chopped

¾ cup small pasta (shells, macaroni, etc.)

1 teaspoon dried basil

1 can (15 ounces) diced tomatoes, Italian or regular, undrained

1 Stir together broth, beans, vegetables, onion, pasta, and basil in a large saucepan.

2 Bring to a boil and reduce heat. Cover and simmer 10 minutes, or until pasta is tender.

3 Stir in tomatoes and heat through.

Makes 10 servings.

TIP:

If you are out of vegetable broth, make your own using 1 tablespoon of **Chicken Style Seasoning** per cup of water.

Per 1 cup serving	Cal	Fat	Sat. Fat	Chol	Sodium	Carbs	Fiber	Sugar	Protein
Something Better	178	1g	0g	0mg	579mg	36g	10g	3g	10g

Meatball Sub

Plan for meatball subs a few days after Spaghetti and Meatballs (page 57) or pull some out of the freezer for a quick and tasty sandwich that's the perfect match for Minestrone.

8 whole wheat sub buns, toasted

1 recipe Pecan Meatballs (page 58)

4 cups Tomato Sauce (page 67) or jar of commercial spaghetti sauce

1 medium onion, thinly sliced

1 medium green pepper, thinly sliced

2 cups soy mozzarella cheese (optional)

1 Fill bun with Pecan Meatballs; cover with sauce.

2 Add onions, peppers, and cheese to sandwich.

3 Toast briefly under broiler to melt cheese, if desired.

Makes 8 sandwiches.

CHANGE IT UP:

Eggplant Parmesan Sub: Use Breaded Eggplant (page 66) in place of Pecan Meatballs.

Per 1 sandwich serving	Cal	Fat	Sat. Fat	Chol	Sodium	Carbs	Fiber	Sugar	Protein
Traditional Recipe	647	30g	0g	73mg	1517mg	64g	0g	0g	28g
Something Better	349	11g	1g	0mg	816mg	51g	10g	8g	14g

menu

White Chili

Avocado Wrap

Tortilla chips with Guilt-Free

Guacamole (page 126)

White Chili

1 tablespoon oil

1 large onion, diced

1 ½ tablespoons minced garlic

4 cans (15 ounces) great northern beans, rinsed and drained

4 cups water

1 can (7 ounces) chopped green chilies

2 tablespoons **Chicken Style Seasoning** (page 152) or commercial brand chicken seasoning

1 ½ teaspoons salt

1 teaspoon dried oregano

½ teaspoon ground cumin

¼ **to** ½ teaspoon cayenne pepper

2 cups Gluten Steaks (page 48), baked and diced, or other **chicken substitute** (page 153)

1 container (8 ounces) commercial **soy sour cream**

White chili is a southwestern favorite, usually made with white meat such as chicken or turkey. We wouldn't let that keep us from enjoying this great spicy and creamy chili—we just used vegetarian "chicken" instead.

1 Heat oil in a large pot over medium. Add onion and garlic; cook until softened, stirring occasionally, about 4 minutes.

2 Add the remaining ingredients, except Gluten Steaks and sour cream, and bring to a boil over high heat.

3 Stir in the Gluten Steaks and sour cream. Reduce to a simmer and cook, uncovered, 30 minutes.

Makes 12 servings.

 TIP:

If you don't have the Gluten Steaks, just leave them out for a great all-bean chili.

Per ¾ cup serving	Cal	Fat	Sat. Fat	Chol	Sodium	Carbs	Fiber	Sugar	Protein
Something Better	277	5g	2g	0mg	429mg	41g	8g	2g	18g

Avocado Wrap

8 whole grain flour tortillas

2 cups Guilt-Free Guacamole (page 126) or commercial brand guacamole

4 cups mixed salad greens or baby spinach leaves

2 large tomatoes, thinly sliced and lightly salted

1 large cucumber, thinly sliced and lightly salted

1 cup matchstick carrots

½ small red onion, thinly sliced

This wrap is a great match for chili because the cool creamy avocado cools down the spiciness of the cayenne pepper.

1 Spread Guilt-Free Guacamole over ¾ of each tortilla, leaving a ½-inch border around the edge.

2 Top with greens, tomatoes, cucumbers, carrots, and onions.

3 Roll up tightly, slice in half, and enjoy!

Makes 8 wraps.

Per 1 wrap serving	Cal	Fat	Sat. Fat	Chol	Sodium	Carbs	Fiber	Sugar	Protein
Something Better	153	3g	0g	0mg	386mg	28g	3g	2g	5g

menu

Lentil Vegetable Soup

Eggless Egg Salad

Lettuce, tomato and red onion

slices for sandwiches

Whole wheat pita bread

Per 1 cup serving	Cal	Fat	Sat. Fat	Chol	Sodium	Carbs	Fiber	Sugar	Protein
Something Better	124	1g	0g	0mg	22mg	21g	7g	3g	7g

Lentil Vegetable Soup

1 tablespoon oil
1 ½ cups shredded cabbage
1 cup carrots, sliced
½ cup celery, diced
½ medium onion, diced
2 cloves garlic, minced
4 cups water
1 ½ cups dry brown lentils
1 cup cut green beans
1 cup frozen peas
4 medium red potatoes, diced
¼ cup **beef style seasoning**
½ tablespoon salt
½ teaspoon dried basil
½ teaspoon dried parsley
1 can (15 ounces) tomatoes, diced
(try Italian-seasoned variety)
1 cup V-8 Juice (low-sodium) or
tomato juice

My mother-in-law and her sister came up with this great soup. Lentils really pack a lot of nutrition into this meal, and with all those vegetables, you have a rainbow in your soup!

1 Heat oil in a large pot over medium heat. Add cabbage, carrots, celery, onion, and garlic; cook until softened, stirring occasionally, about 5 minutes.
2 Add water, lentils, green beans, peas, potatoes, beef style seasoning, salt, basil, and parsley to pot.
3 Bring to a boil over high heat. Reduce to a simmer and cook until lentils are softened, about 45 minutes.
4 Add tomatoes and V-8 juice; simmer 15 minutes.
Makes 16 servings.

TIP:

No V-8 Juice? Just use a 15-ounce can of tomato sauce mixed with a little water.

SHORTCUT:

Use frozen mixed vegetables instead of fresh.

Eggless Egg Salad

2 packages (14 ounces) water-packed
tofu, firm or extra-firm, well drained
4 stalks celery, finely diced
½ small onion, finely diced
½ cup **pickle relish**
½ cup Aioli (page 130) or
commercial **soy mayonnaise**
1 tablespoon **Chicken Style Seasoning**
(page 152) or commercial brand
chicken seasoning
1 ½ teaspoons garlic powder
1 to 1 ½ teaspoons salt
1 teaspoon onion powder
¼ teaspoon turmeric
(optional, for color)

My daughter loves this stuff—she would eat it every day if I let her!

1 Drain excess water from tofu. (See "How To" on page 150)
2 Mash tofu in a large bowl with a fork or potato masher.
3 Add remaining ingredients and mix well. Chill before serving.
Makes 15 servings.

TIP:

We love to use **pickles** cured with lemon juice-the flavor is so much better than traditional vinegar pickles. See page 166.

Per ⅓ cup serving	Cal	Fat	Sat. Fat	Chol	Sodium	Carbs	Fiber	Sugar	Protein
Egg Salad	235	22g	4g	229mg	268mg	1g	0g	1g	8g
Something Better	**119**	**9g**	**0g**	**0mg**	**219mg**	**4g**	**1g**	**0g**	**7g**

menu

Split Pea Soup

Chicken Salad

Lettuce, tomato and red onion slices

for sandwiches

All American Salad (page 26)

Per 1 cup serving	Cal	Fat	Sat. Fat	Chol	Sodium	Carbs	Fiber	Sugar	Protein
Something Better	149	0g	0g	0mg	896mg	31g	5g	1g	5g

Split Pea Soup

12 cups water

4 cups split peas

4 medium potatoes, diced (optional)

3 ribs celery, chopped

2 medium carrots, peeled and chopped

1 medium onion, chopped

4 teaspoons salt

2 teaspoons minced garlic, or

1 teaspoon garlic powder

½ teaspoon dried thyme

½ teaspoon dried marjoram

2 bay leaves

It's green, so it has to be good for you, right? Right! Split peas have so many good qualities I can't even list them all here! They are high in protein, B vitamins, and isoflavones, with virtually no fat! They are also high in fiber, which can help lower cholesterol and stabilize blood sugar. And if that is not reason enough to try this soup, it is really easy to make!

1 Combine all ingredients in a large saucepan.

2 Bring to a boil over high heat; lower to a simmer and cook 60 to 90 minutes, until split peas are tender.

Makes 12 servings.

 TIP:

Make it even easier! Combine everything in a slow cooker in the morning, and let it cook on high for 8 hours. It's ready just in time for dinner!

Chicken Salad

3 cups prepared **Soy Curls** (page 150), cooled, gluten steaks (page 48) or other **chicken substitute**

¼ medium onion, finely diced

3 stalks celery, diced

½ cup **pickle relish** (page 166)

½ cup Aioli (page 130) or commercial **soy mayonnaise**

1 tablespoon **Chicken Style Seasoning** (page 152) or commercial brand chicken seasoning

1 ½ teaspoons garlic powder

1 ½ teaspoons salt

1 teaspoon onion powder

Now you can enjoy this picnic classic with a healthy twist! Our recipe for chicken salad has none of the risks of the disease that chicken potentially carries, and it has all the health benefits of soy!

1 Place prepared Soy Curls in a food processor; pulse until slightly chunky.

2 Add remaining ingredients to food processor; mix well. Chill well before serving.

3 Serve on your favorite bread or pita with lettuce, tomato, and red onion slices.

Makes 12 servings.

 TIP:

Make any chicken salad recipe vegetarian by simply subbing in **Soy Curls**. Easy!

 SHORTCUT:

Put this recipe together quickly by using a commercial **chicken substitute**.

Per ⅓ cup serving	Cal	Fat	Sat. Fat	Chol	Sodium	Carbs	Fiber	Sugar	Protein
Traditional Recipe	139	11g	2g	33mg	96mg	1g	0g	0g	10g
Something Better	**113**	**9g**	**0g**	**0mg**	**345mg**	**4g**	**1g**	**0g**	**4g**

menu

Gluten Steaks

Also known as "wheat meat," gluten is a meat substitute that comes from the protein portion of wheat. It's a great substitute when moving to a more plant-based diet because of its meaty texture and flavor.

GLUTEN DOUGH

2 ½ cups **gluten flour** (shake down into measuring cup before leveling)

½ cup quick-cooking oats

⅓ cup **nutritional yeast flakes**

¼ cup raw wheat germ

2 tablespoons **Chicken Style Seasoning** (page 152) or commercial brand chicken seasoning

1 tablespoon onion powder

1 teaspoon garlic powder

½ teaspoon salt

⅛ teaspoon cayenne pepper

2 cups water

BROTH

13 cups water

¾ cups **Braggs Liquid Aminos** or low sodium soy sauce

1 tablespoon onion powder

¼ cup **Chicken Style Seasoning** (page 152) or commercial brand

¼ teaspoon cayenne pepper

½ teaspoon garlic powder

GLUTEN DOUGH & BROTH

1 Mix all ingredients, except water, together in a large mixing bowl.

2 Add water and stir quickly; gently knead for 1 minute.

3 Shape dough into a log; wrap in plastic and refrigerate anywhere from 1 hour to overnight.

4 Combine all broth ingredients in a large pot; bring to a boil over high heat.

5 Cut chilled dough into thin ¼-inch slices; gently place into boiling broth, being careful not stack on top of each other.

6 Reduce heat to a low simmer; cover and cook 45 minutes. Allow to cool in broth, or bake immediately. May be frozen at this point for later use.

GLUTEN STEAKS

1 Preheat oven to 400°F. Coat a large baking sheet with non-stick cooking spray or line with parchment paper.

2 Dip prepared gluten dough in breading mix; (page 151) place on prepared baking sheet.

3 Lightly coat gluten dough with non-stick cooking spray.

4 Bake 15 minutes; turn and bake an additional 15 minutes, or until golden brown.

Makes 12 servings.

TIP:

Use as a **chicken substitute** in recipes by skipping step 2. After baking, use in recipes such as Chicken Stew (page 56), Tater Tot Casserole (page 106), Mexican Chicken (page 79), or any of your recipes that call for cooked chicken.

Per 2 piece serving	Cal	Fat	Sat. Fat	Chol	Sodium	Carbs	Fiber	Sugar	Protein
Breaded Chicken	462	28g	6g	84mg	872mg	25g	1g	1g	24g
Something Better	**113**	**9g**	**0g**	**0mg**	**345mg**	**4g**	**1g**	**0g**	**4g**

menu

Vegetable Pot Pie

Pie Crust Crackers

Cobb Salad (page 26)

Vegetable Pot Pie

Remember those frozen pot pies you ate when you were a kid? Everybody loved them—it is comfort food at its best. Keep the tradition alive! Many kids these days have never had pot pie. Don't deprive your kids of this tradition—make Pot Pie today!

SAVORY PIE CRUST

½ cup warm water

½ cup oil

1 cup whole wheat flour

1 cup quick-cooking oats, blended until fine

1 teaspoon salt

1 Beat water and oil together in a small bowl with a fork or small whisk.

2 Mix flours and salt together in a separate medium bowl.

3 Add oil mixture to flour mixture, stirring until dough is just formed. Do not overmix because the crust will be tough.

4 Roll dough between wax paper or plastic wrap. See page 150 for more details on rolling out pie crust.

Makes one 9-by-13-inch pie or two 9-inch pies.

FILLING

7 cups potatoes, diced

2 cups carrots, sliced

2 cups onions, chopped

3 cups frozen peas or mixed vegetables

GRAVY

4 cups **nondairy milk**, unsweetened

⅓ cup Country-Style Seasoning (page 152) or commercial brand **Chicken Style Seasoning**

¼ cup cornstarch

2 tablespoons onion powder

½ teaspoon salt

FILLING & GRAVY

1 Preheat oven to 350°F.

2 Combine potatoes, carrots, and onions in a large pot; add water to cover and salt well. Bring to a boil over high heat; cook until vegetables are tender.

3 Drain and return to pot.

4 Combine all gravy ingredients in a blender; puree until smooth.

5 Pour mixture into a medium saucepan; bring to a boil over high heat. Boil 1 minute, until thick, stirring constantly.

6 Add gravy and frozen vegetables to potato mixture in pot; stir gently to mix.

7 Spread mixture into a 9-by-13-inch casserole dish or two 8-inch pie pans.

8 Top with prepared crust and bake 1 hour.

Makes 12 servings.

NOW & LATER:

Prepare filling and crust separately up to a day ahead. If you roll out the crust and leave it between the plastic wrap, it folds up nicely and you can just put it on the pie before baking.

Per 1 piece serving	Cal	Fat	Sat. Fat	Chol	Sodium	Carbs	Fiber	Sugar	Protein
Traditional Recipe	484	29g	8g	41mg	857mg	43g	2g	8g	13g
Something Better	**332**	**8g**	**1g**	**0mg**	**295mg**	**58g**	**9g**	**6g**	**11g**

menu

Special T Loaf

Brown Gravy (page 128)

or Ketchup (page 130)

Cheezie Potatoes (Page 119)

Steamed green beans

All-American Salad (page 26)

Special T Loaf

You can't go to an Adventist potluck without having a Special T Loaf—it's the vegetarian family's meat loaf. But don't let the name "loaf" fool you! If you make it in a loaf pan, it will be too thick and won't get cook properly in the middle.

1 tablespoon oil

1 cup onion, diced

1 cup celery, diced

2 packages (12.3 ounces) Mori Nu **tofu**, firm

1 cup pecan meal

1 cup walnuts, finely chopped

¼ cup oil

¼ cup **nutritional yeast flakes**

1 tablespoon **Chicken Style Seasoning** (page 152) or commercial brand chicken seasoning

1 ½ teaspoons salt

7 cups rice flake cereal (about 1 12-ounce box)

1 to 1 ½ cups soy milk, unsweetened, as needed

1. Preheat oven to 350°F. Lightly coat a 9-by-13-inch casserole dish with non-stick cooking spray.

2. Heat oil in a medium skillet over medium. Add onion and celery; cook until translucent, stirring occasionally, about 4 minutes.

3. Transfer onion mixture to a large bowl; add remaining ingredients, except rice flake cereal and milk, and mix well.

4. Add rice flake cereal; mix gently. Add milk as needed to moisten the mixture until it sticks together.

5. Press mixture evenly into prepared dish. Cover and bake 40 minutes.

6. Remove cover and bake an additional 15 minutes, until browned and crispy on the edges.

Makes 16 pieces.

NOW & LATER:

Make a double batch of this recipe and freeze it before baking. Next time you're ready for a Special T loaf, simply allow it to thaw completely, and then bake as directed.

TIP:

If you don't have pecan meal, grind pecans in a food processor until fine. Then you can quickly chop the onions and celery in the food processor as well.

Per 1 piece serving	Cal	Fat	Sat. Fat	Chol	Sodium	Carbs	Fiber	Sugar	Protein
Meatloaf	220	13g	4g	85mg	447mg	7g	0g	2g	17g
Something Better	**224**	**15g**	**2g**	**0mg**	**314mg**	**14g**	**2g**	**3g**	**10g**

menu

Oatmeal Patties

Mushroom Gravy (page 128)

Roasted Garlic Potatoes (page 120, variation)

or Baked sweet potato

Green Bean Casserole (page 118)

All-American Salad (page 26)

Oatmeal Patties

Oatmeal isn't just for breakfast! Our oatmeal patties are loaded with healthy omega 3 fats, and they were a favorite in our test kitchens. Serve with brown gravy or mushroom gravy—you can't go wrong.

1 ½ cup water

⅓ cup ground **flax seeds**

1 medium onion, cut into large pieces

½ cup walnuts, lightly toasted

3 cups quick-cooking oats

3 tablespoons **beef style seasoning**

1 ½ tablespoons **Chicken Style Seasoning** (page 152) or commercial brand chicken seasoning

½ teaspoon salt

1 package (8 ounces) baby portabella mushrooms, chopped (optional)

2 to 4 tablespoons oil, as needed

1 Mix water and flax seeds together in a small bowl; set aside.

2 Combine onion and walnuts in a food processor; pulse until minced.

3 Add remaining ingredients, except mushrooms, to food processor; pulse until combined.

4 Add mushrooms to food processor; pulse until finely chopped.

5 Form mixture into patties using a ¼-cup measuring cup.

6 Heat a large skillet over medium; add enough oil to make a thin layer over the surface of the skillet. Add patties to skillet; cook until golden brown on both sides, about 10 minutes total.

Makes 8 servings.

NOW & LATER:

Make an extra batch of the recipe, then freeze them for later use or save them for burgers on your "Junk Food Day."

CHANGE IT UP:

Serve these cooked patties in buns with burger toppings.

Per 2 patty serving	Cal	Fat	Sat. Fat	Chol	Sodium	Carbs	Fiber	Sugar	Protein
Chopped Steak	618	54g	23g	142mg	136mg	0g	0g	0g	33g
Something Better	**209**	**9g***	**0g**	**0mg**	**686mg**	**25g**	**6g**	**1g**	**7g**

*The fat in this recipe comes from the "good for you" omega-3 fats in the flax seeds and walnuts

Menu

Chicken Stew

Served over whole grain biscuits, this is a great southern-style meal that people love.

1 tablespoon oil

1 medium onion, finely minced

1 cup celery, diced

1 cup carrots, diced

2 cups potatoes, peeled and diced

2 cups frozen mixed vegetables

6 cups water

3 ½ tablespoons **Chicken Style Seasoning** (page 152) or commercial chicken seasoning

½ teaspoon salt

1 tablespoon dried parsley

1 cup **chicken substitute** (page 153) or Gluten Steaks (page 48)

1 cup cold **nondairy milk**, unsweetened

⅓ cup cornstarch

1 Heat oil in a large skillet over medium. Add onion and cook until translucent, stirring occasionally, about 3 minutes.

2 Add celery and carrots to skillet; cook until softened, about 4 minutes, stirring occasionally. Add remaining ingredients, except milk and cornstarch. Simmer until all vegetables are tender.

3 Combine milk and cornstarch in a small bowl; mix until smooth. Stir into cooked vegetables and simmer five minutes, until thickened.

Makes 12 servings.

 CHANGE IT UP:

Chicken Pot Pie: Use ½ cup of cornstarch instead of ⅓ cup, and top it with the Savory Pie Crust (page 50) for an old family favorite.

Per ¾ cup serving	Cal	Fat	Sat. Fat	Chol	Sodium	Carbs	Fiber	Sugar	Protein
Beef Stew	252	9g	2g	50mg	444mg	19g	2g	1g	23g
Something Better	**178**	**2g**	**0g**	**0mg**	**257mg**	**27g**	**5g**	**2g**	**14g**

Easy Biscuits

DRY INGREDIENTS

3 cups **whole wheat pastry flour**

3 tablespoons **cane juice crystals** or sugar

1 tablespoon **aluminum-free baking powder**

¼ teaspoon salt

WET INGREDIENTS

1 cup **nondairy milk**, unsweetened

⅓ cup oil

1 Preheat oven to 425°F. Coat muffin tins with non-stick cooking spray.

2 Mix dry ingredients together. Mix wet ingredients together in a separate small bowl.

3 Add wet ingredients to dry ingredients; mix until just combined.

4 If batter seems too thick, add more milk, 1 tablespoon at a time, until batter comes together. The batter should be thick, like brownie batter.

5 Fill prepared muffin tins with batter; bake 10 minutes, or until light brown.

Makes 12 biscuits.

menu

Spaghetti and Meatballs

Thin spaghetti, cooked

Tomato Sauce (page 67)

or jar of commercial spaghetti sauce

Pecan Meatballs

Steamed green beans

Italian Salad (page 25)

Garlic Bread (see TIP)

Per 5 meatball serving	Cal	Fat	Sat. Fat	Chol	Sodium	Carbs	Fiber	Sugar	Protein
Traditional Recipe	283	18g	7g	104mg	669mg	11g	1g	2g	17g
Something Better	**152**	**8g**	**0g**	**0mg**	**191mg**	**17g**	**4g**	**3g**	**5g**

Pecan meatballs

Meat-free meatballs—is it possible? It sure is! These yummy little meatballs hold up nicely in sauce and add great texture to your spaghetti dinner!

4 cups soft whole grain bread crumbs (approximately 8 slices bread)

1 cup quick-cooking oats

1 cup pecan meal

1 cup onion, cut into large pieces

1 cup celery, cut into large pieces

½ cup water

1 teaspoon **Braggs Liquid Aminos** or low sodium soy sauce

½ teaspoon dried oregano

½ teaspoon paprika

½ teaspoon garlic powder

½ teaspoon salt

1 Preheat oven to 350°F. Lightly coat a large baking sheet with non-stick cooking spray.

2 Combine bread crumbs, oats, and pecan meal in a large bowl. Set aside.

3 Combine remaining ingredients in food processor; process until finely ground.

4 Add mixture to dry ingredients; stir until thoroughly mixed. Let mixture sit for 5 minutes to absorb moisture.

5 Form mixture into 1-inch balls, pressing firmly with hands to shape balls well; place on prepared baking sheet.

6 Bake until browned, about 30 minutes, turning meatballs over halfway through.

Makes 12 servings.

NOW & LATER:

These meatballs freeze well, so double or triple this recipe and you'll have some ready for next time, or plan for Meatball Subs (page 40) later in the week.

SHORTCUT:

Use commercial spaghetti sauce and vegetarian burger crumbles to make Spaghetti and Meat Sauce.

TIP:

Make sure you press your meatballs together firmly as you form them so they don't fall apart in your sauce.

TIP:

Garlinc Bread: Cut a multi-grain baguette in half and spread with **non-hydrogenated margarine**. Sprinkle with garlic salt and parsley; bake at 350°F until toasted. Or use the Garlic Spread (page 64) and toast.

menu

Pasta Primavera or CHANGE IT UP

Spinach Salad (page 25)

Garlic Bread (see TIP)

Pasta Primavera

You won't miss any of the fat or calories in this version of pasta primavera. The rich creamy Alfredo sauce makes this vegetable filled pasta dish one your whole family will enjoy!

1 tablespoon oil
½ cup carrot, julienned
½ cup onion, thinly sliced
½ cup red or yellow bell pepper, sliced
2 cups cauliflower florets
1 bunch broccoli florets
1 medium zucchini or yellow squash, sliced
½ to 1 teaspoon salt
1 box (16 ounces) penne pasta, cooked according to package directions
1 recipe Alfredo Sauce (page 68)
1 cup tomatoes, diced
¼ cup **nondairy parmesan cheese** or **nutritional yeast flakes** (optional)

1 Heat oil in a large skillet over medium. Add onion, carrot, and bell pepper; cook until softened, about 4 minutes.

2 Add cauliflower, broccoli, zucchini, and salt to skillet; cook until vegetables are tender, stirring occasionally, about 5 minutes.

3 Add pasta and sauce to skillet; mix gently and cook until heated through.

4 Top with tomatoes and nondairy parmesan cheese, if using.

Makes 8 servings.

 CHANGE IT UP:

Pesto Pasta: Add ⅛ to ¼ cup of Basil Pesto (page 129) to Alfredo Sauce (page 68).

CHANGE IT UP:

Fettuccini Alfredo: Top pasta with Alfredo Sauce (page 68) and serve with steamed vegetables on the side.

 SHORTCUT:

Use pre-cut or frozen vegetables.

 TIP*:

Garlic Bread: Cut a multi-grain baguette in half and spread with **non-hydrogenated margarine**. Sprinkle with garlic salt and parsley; bake at 350°F until toasted. Or use the Garlic Spread (page 64) and toast.

Per 1 ½ cup serving	Cal	Fat	Sat. Fat	Chol	Sodium	Carbs	Fiber	Sugar	Protein
Traditional Recipe	350	9g	3g	15mg	740mg	51g	4g	9g	11g
Something Better	**326**	**5g**	**0g**	**0mg**	**434mg**	**51g**	**5g**	**4g**	**16g**

menu

Lasagna or CHANGE IT UP

Italian Salad (page 25)

Steamed broccoli

Ciabatta bread with dipping sauce (see TIP)

Lasagna

We have Lasagna for Christmas dinner because it is easier to put together than a traditional dinner and everyone loves it. This version is so good, your whole family will love it! If you have a real meat lover in the family, try adding some vegetarian Italian sausage to one of the layers and he'll be more than satisfied!

6 cups Tomato Sauce (page 67) or jar of commercial spaghetti sauce

12 lasagna noodles, cooked

1 recipe Tofu Ricotta (page 68)

¼ cup **nondairy parmesan cheese** (optional)

1 Preheat oven to 350°F. Lightly coat a 9-by-13-inch baking dish with non-stick cooking spray.

2 Ladle 1 ½ cups Tomato Sauce in the bottom of the prepared dish. Arrange 4 noodles over the sauce. Spread ½ of the Tofu Ricotta over the noodles. Repeat layers once.

3 Top with remaining 4 noodles and cover with remaining sauce. Sprinkle with parmesan, if using.

4 Cover with aluminum foil and bake 1 hour.

Makes 16 servings or one 9-by-13-inch dish.

 CHANGE IT UP:

Stuffed Jumbo Shells (Manicotti): Ladle Tomato Sauce into the bottom of the baking dish; place prepared Jumbo Shells or Manicotti, filled with Tofu Ricotta, on top. Cover with additional sauce and bake until bubbly.

 CHANGE IT UP:

Meaty Lasagna: Add a layer of vegetarian Italian sausage in the middle of the Lasagna.

 SHORTCUT:

Use a jar of commercial spaghetti sauce, Tofutti Sour Cream (in place of the Aioli in the Tofu Ricotta), and oven-ready noodles for a lasagna that comes together in a flash.

TIP:

Dipping Sauce: Mix olive oil with your favorite Italian herbs and serve in a shallow dish for dipping.

Per 1 piece serving	Cal	Fat	Sat. Fat	Chol	Sodium	Carbs	Fiber	Sugar	Protein
Traditional Recipe	336	12g	6g	49mg	744mg	35g	3g	6g	21g
Something Better	**277**	**6g**	**1g**	**0mg**	**515mg**	**45g**	**3g**	**5g**	**11g**

menu

Pasta with Spring Vegetables

Spinach Salad (page 25)

Italian Bread with Garlic Spread (see TIP)

Pasta with Spring Vegetables

Okay, you caught me...I don't just make this in the spring! It's so good you'll want to have it all year around, so just use whatever veggies are in season.

2 tablespoons oil

½ cup red onion, diced

2 cloves garlic, minced

4 stalks celery, diced

1 cup carrot, diced

1 pound fresh asparagus, green beans, or broccoli, cut into 1-inch pieces, or

1 cup leafy greens

1 medium zucchini, diced

2 teaspoons salt

2 cups vegetable broth or

2 cups of broth made from **Chicken Style Seasoning** (page 165)

½ tablespoon cornstarch

1 package (14 ounce) whole grain angel hair pasta, cooked according to package directions

2 cups tomatoes, diced or grape tomatoes

6 to 10 leaves fresh basil leaves, or

1 teaspoon dried basil

½ teaspoon dried oregano

dash cayenne pepper, to taste (optional)

1 Heat oil in a large skillet over medium. Add onion, garlic, celery, and carrots; cook until softened, stirring occasionally, about 8 minutes.

2 Add asparagus, zucchini, and salt to skillet; cook until vegetables are just softened, about 4 minutes.

3 Meanwhile, whisk broth and cornstarch together in a small bowl.

4 Add broth and remaining ingredients to skillet; bring to a boil over high heat and cook until slightly thickened.

Makes 8 servings.

TIP:

Use vegetables that your family enjoys.

SHORTCUT:

Save time chopping all those vegetables by using pre-cut vegetables from the produce isle. Frozen vegetables work great too!

TIP:

Garlic Spread: Mix non-hydrogenated margarine with a generous amount of minced garlic and a sprinkle of parsley.

Per 1 ½ cup serving	Cal	Fat	Sat. Fat	Chol	Sodium	Carbs	Fiber	Sugar	Protein
Something Better	261	4g	0g	0mg	655mg	47g	5g	5g	9g

menu

Eggplant Parmesan or CHANGE IT UP

Italian Salad (page 25)

Garlic Bread (see TIP page 60)

Per serving	Cal	Fat	Sat. Fat	Chol	Sodium	Carbs	Fiber	Sugar	Protein
Traditional Recipe	317	22g	9g	55mg	604mg	17g	4g	5g	14g
Something Better	**355**	**7g**	**0g**	**0mg**	**407mg**	**58g**	**5g**	**3g**	**12g**

Eggplant Parmesan

A favorite at Italian restaurants everywhere, made cheaper and healthier at home. Many of us say we don't like eggplant, but all the eggplant haters I know love this recipe. The crispy outer layer gives it a nice crunch, and it's perfect with a good tomato sauce.

EGGPLANT PARMESAN

1 package (14 ounces) whole grain angel hair pasta, cooked according to package directions

1 recipe Breaded Eggplant

4 cups Tomato Sauce (page 67) or jar of commercial spaghetti sauce

½ cup **nondairy parmesan cheese**

BREADED EGGPLANT

2 medium eggplants, peeled and cut into ⅓-inch thick slices

2 cups Breading Mix (page 151) or commercial breading mix

BATTER

½ cup Aioli (page 130) or commercial **soy mayonnaise**

¼ **to** ½ cup water

1 Serve eggplant on a bed of pasta, covered with sauce and a sprinkling of parmesan cheese.

Makes 8 servings.

BREADED EGGPLANT

1 Preheat oven to 350°F. Lightly coat a large baking sheet with non-stick cooking spray.

2 Mix batter ingredients together in a small bowl; set aside. Place Breading Mix in a shallow dish.

3 Dip eggplant into the batter, then into the breading. Place breaded eggplant onto prepared baking sheet.

4 Lightly spray the tops of the eggplant with non-stick cooking spray. Bake 15 minutes on each side, or until browned and crispy.

Makes 16 servings.

 NOW & LATER:

Make an extra batch and use it in an Eggplant Sub (page 40, variation) later this week.

 SHORTCUT:

Use commercial chicken patties such as Boca in place of the Breaded Eggplant.

CHANGE IT UP:

Chicken Parmesan: Use Gluten Steaks (page 48) in place of the eggplant.

 TIP:

These are great prepared ahead of time. Just warm them in a single layer on a baking sheet—they get even crisper.

Per 2 piece serving	Cal	Fat	Sat. Fat	Chol	Sodium	Carbs	Fiber	Sugar	Protein
Something Better	59	5g	0g	0mg	44mg	3g	2g	1g	0g

Tomato Sauce

I love this Tomato Sauce. It is so versatile that it has become a staple in many of my favorite meals. This recipe is lower in fat and sugar than most commercial brands, but it is still rich and full of flavor. I like to make a big batch and freeze half for later.

2 tablespoons oil

1 large onion, chopped

1 cup green bell pepper, chopped (optional)

8 cloves garlic, minced

2 tablespoons dried basil

1 tablespoon dried oregano

1 tablespoon salt

5 cans (28 ounces) tomatoes (any kind will work—crushed, diced, pureed, or sauce)

2 tablespoons maple syrup or other sweetener

1 Heat oil in a large stock pot over medium. Add onion, bell pepper, and garlic; cook until onions are translucent, stirring occasionally, about 5 minutes.

2 Add basil, oregano, and salt to stock pot; cook 2 minutes, stirring occasionally.

3 Add tomatoes and maple syrup to stock pot; stir well. Add water if needed.

4 Bring to a boil over high heat; lower to a simmer and cook 1 hour.

Makes 12 cups.

 NOW & LATER:

Freeze half of this recipe so you are one step ahead the next time you make an Italian meal.

Per ½ cup serving	Cal	Fat	Sat. Fat	Chol	Sodium	Carbs	Fiber	Sugar	Protein
Traditional Recipe	70	2.5	0g	0mg	480mg	10g	2g	6g	2g
Something Better	**50**	**1g**	**0g**	**0mg**	**360mg**	**9g**	**2g**	**1g**	**2g**

Alfredo Sauce

Smooth and creamy Alfredo Sauce is great change of pace from traditional Tomato Sauce when it is "Italian day." Or, do what my husband does and put both on your spaghetti.

1 package (12.3 ounces) Mori Nu
Silken **tofu**, firm

1 ½ cups **nondairy milk**, unsweetened

½ teaspoon garlic, minced

1 tablespoon olive oil

3 tablespoons vegan parmesan cheese
or **nutritional yeast flakes**

1 teaspoon salt

1 teaspoon onion powder

1 teaspoon dried basil

1 teaspoon dried parsley

1 Place tofu, nondairy milk, garlic, oil, cheese, salt, and onion powder in a blender; blend until smooth and creamy.

2 Add basil, parsley, and salt; stir gently.

3 Pour mixture into a medium saucepan; cook until heated through over medium heat.
Makes 6 servings.

 TIP:

Do not boil or bake!
Your sauce will curdle.

Per ½ cup serving	Cal	Fat	Sat. Fat	Chol	Sodium	Carbs	Fiber	Sugar	Protein
Traditional Recipe	220	20g	10g	80mg	920mg	6g	0g	2g	2g
Something Better	**92**	**4g**	**0g**	**0mg**	**372mg**	**4g**	**0g**	**0g**	**7g**

Tofu Ricotta

2 packages (14 ounces) water-packed
tofu, firm or extra-firm

1 package (16 ounces) frozen spinach,
thawed and drained (optional)

1 cup Aioli (page 130) or commercial
soy sour cream or **soy mayonnaise**

¼ cup lemon juice

¼ cup **cane juice crystals** or
other sweetener

1 ¼ teaspoons salt

¾ teaspoon onion powder

¾ teaspoon garlic powder

Taste it…adjust the seasonings if you need to. If it tastes good plain, it will be GREAT in the lasagna.

1 Drain excess water from tofu. (See "How To" on page 150)

2 Mash tofu in a large bowl with a potato masher or your hands.

3 Add remaining ingredients to tofu; mix well. Add additional salt or sweetener if needed.
Makes 16 servings.

menu

Bean and Rice Chimichanga

Shredded lettuce

Diced tomatoes

Aioli (page 130) or commercial **soy sour cream**

Guilt-Free Guacamole (page 126) or commercial

guacamole

Tortilla Chips and Salsa (page 32)

Bean and Rice Chimichanga

I used to eat at a Mexican restaurant where they served a deep-fried burrito called a chimichanga. Obviously that isn't a good choice now that I am trying to be healthier, so what should I do? Give up one of my favorites? No, not me. I just found a way to make it "better"!

10 burrito-size whole grain flour tortillas
1 recipe Refried Beans (page 79) or
2 cans (15 ounces) vegetarian refried beans
1 recipe Cilantro Lime Rice (page 123, variation) or Spanish Rice (page 124)
1 cup Salsa (page 32) or commercial salsa
½ cup onion, diced

1 Preheat oven to 400°F. Lightly coat a large baking sheet with non-stick cooking spray.
2 Put about ⅓ cup beans and ¼ cup rice into each tortilla.
3 Add 2 tablespoons Salsa and 1 tablespoon onion into each tortilla.
4 Wrap each burrito and put seam side down on prepared baking sheet.
5 Coat burritos lightly with cooking spray; bake 15 minutes. Turn over and bake an additional 10 minutes, until golden brown.

Makes 10 chimichangas.

 CHANGE IT UP:

Wet Burritos: Place prepared burritos in a 9-by-13-inch baking dish. Cover with Salsa (page 32) or enchilada sauce; bake until sauce is hot and bubbly, about 30 minutes.

Per 1 chimichanga	Cal	Fat	Sat. Fat	Chol	Sodium	Carbs	Fiber	Sugar	Protein
Traditional Recipe	443	23g	11g	51mg	957mg	39g	3g	2g	20g
Something Better	**324**	**5g**	**1g**	**0mg**	**662mg**	**54g**	**11g**	**3g**	**15g**

menu

Chilaquiles

Aioli (page 130) or commercial **soy sour cream**

Green onions

Cucumber, Tomato, Avocado Salad (page 32)

Corn or Oven Roasted Potatoes (page 120)

Chilaquiles

Chilaquiles is one of my personal favorites! It's a Tex-Mex dish created to use up leftover tortillas for a traditional Mexican breakfast, but I like to eat it for a main meal. The only problem with this recipe is liking it too much, if you know what I mean!

4 tablespoons oil

1 cup onion, diced

5 cloves garlic, minced

1 cup Gluten Steaks (page 48) or other **chicken or beef substitute**, diced

1 package (14 ounces) tofu, firm, crumbled, or **2** cups Scrambled Tofu (page 10)

½ small jalapeno, diced (optional)

12 corn tortillas, torn into medium size pieces

1 ½ cups tomatoes, diced or commercial salsa

¼ cup fresh cilantro, chopped

1 Heat 1 tablespoon oil in a large skillet over medium. Add onions and garlic; cook until tender, about 2 minutes. Add meat substitute, tofu, and jalapeno; cook 3 minutes, stirring occasionally.

2 Heat remaining 3 tablespoons oil in a large skillet over medium.

3 Drop torn tortillas into the hot oil; cook about 4 minutes, stirring often to cook evenly.

4 When tortillas are lightly browned and crispy, add reserved tofu mixture, tomatoes, and cilantro; mix well. Serve immediately.

Makes 6 servings.

TIP:

You can make this meal lower in fat by wrapping the filling in the tortillas instead of tearing and frying them. It's a different dish, but it is really good.

CHANGE IT UP:

Southwestern Breakfast Scramble: Leave out the tortillas and use a vegetarian breakfast sausage in place of the meat substitute.

Per 1 cup serving	Cal	Fat	Sat. Fat	Chol	Sodium	Carbs	Fiber	Sugar	Protein
Traditional Recipe	438	31g	9g	197mg	541mg	27g	4g	5g	13g
Something Better	**228**	**10g**	**0g**	**0mg**	**112mg**	**28g**	**5g**	**3g**	**9g**

menu

Veggie Burrito

Shredded lettuce

Diced tomatoes

Black olives

Salsa (page 32) or commercial salsa

Aioli (page 130) or commercial **soy sour cream**

Guilt-Free Guacamole (page 126)

or commercial guacamole

Tortilla chips

Veggie Burrito

My whole family loves Mexican food, especially burritos. You can make a burrito anyway you like, but this version is a copy-cat recipe from a favorite restaurant.

10 burrito-size whole grain flour tortillas
1 recipe Black Beans (page 80),
Refried Beans (page 79), or
2 cans vegetarian refried beans
1 recipe Roasted Fajita
Veggies (page 76)
1 ½ cups Salsa (page 32) or
commercial salsa
¾ cup onion, diced

1 Warm tortillas to soften.
2 Place ½ cup beans and ⅓ cup Roasted Fajita Veggies on each tortilla.
3 Add 2 tablespoons Salsa and 1 tablespoon onion.
4 Wrap up the burrito or better yet, let everybody make their own!
Makes 10 burritos.

CHANGE IT UP:

Make it "Meaty" by adding Mexican Chicken (page 79) or Taco Burger (page 78) with your veggies.

SHORTCUT:

Make simple bean burritos with canned beans and commercial salsa for a quick and hearty meal. Serve with some fresh vegetables or fruit for a complete meal.

CHANGE IT UP:

Make this a Chimichanga simply by following the baking instructions for the Bean and Rice Chimichanga (page 70). Or make wet burritos by placing prepared burritos in a 9-by-13-inch pan. Cover with Salsa or enchilada sauce and bake in a 350°F oven 20 to 30 minutes, until sauce is hot and bubbly, about 30 minutes.

Per 1 burrito serving	Cal	Fat	Sat. Fat	Chol	Sodium	Carbs	Fiber	Sugar	Protein
Beef Burrito	721	33g	12g	121mg	1314mg	56g	3g	2g	45g
Something Better	**241**	**4g**	**1g**	**0mg**	**828mg**	**40g**	**10g**	**4g**	**13g**

menu

Veggie Fajitas

Shredded lettuce

Diced tomatoes

Salsa (page 32) or commercial salsa

Aioli (page 130) or commercial **soy sour cream**

Guilt-Free Guacamole (page 126) or commercial

guacamole

Tortilla chips

Spanish Rice (page 124)

or Cilantro Lime Rice (page 123)

Veggie Fajitas

As far as I can tell, these are just grown up tacos! But they are not just for grown-ups—kids love them, too!

1 recipe Refried Beans (page 79) or
2 cans vegetarian refried beans
1 recipe Roasted Fajita Veggies (recipe below)
1 recipe Mexican Chicken (page 79) (optional)
1 to 2 bags whole grain tortillas, soft taco size

1 Warm tortillas to soften. Keep warm by wrapping in a lint-free dish towel.
2 Fill each tortilla with Refried Beans, Roasted Fajita Veggies and Mexican Chicken.
Makes 12 fajitas.

 SHORTCUT:
Use a commercial **chicken substitute** in place of Mexican Chicken.

 SHORTCUT:
Canned refried beans work great. Look for the fat-free or vegetarian variety and mix in some salsa to give the beans a nice flavor.

Per 1 fajita serving	Cal	Fat	Sat. Fat	Chol	Sodium	Carbs	Fiber	Sugar	Protein
Traditional Recipe	377	16g	5g	36mg	827mg	33g	3g	4g	24g
Something Better	**216**	**4g**	**0g**	**0mg**	**439mg**	**36g**	**8g**	**2g**	**10g**

Roasted Fajita Veggies

1 medium onion, cut into thin strips
1 medium green pepper, cut into thin strips
1 medium red pepper, cut into thin strips
1 ½ tablespoons oil
1 tablespoons lemon or lime juice
1 teaspoon garlic, minced
1 to 2 tablespoons Taco Seasoning (page 151) or ½ to 1 tablespoon commercial taco seasoning
¼ cup fresh cilantro, coarsely chopped (optional)

We like to oven-roast our veggies for great flavor. This recipe is so similar to the Mexican Chicken that you can make them together in the oven or even on the stove top if you like.

1 Preheat oven to 400°F. Lightly coat a large baking sheet with non-stick cooking spray.
2 Mix all the ingredients, except cilantro, in a large bowl or zip lock bag until coated. Spread mixture onto prepared baking sheet.
3 Bake 20 to 25 minutes, until vegetables are tender, stirring after 10 minutes.
4 Stir in cilantro, if using, just before serving.
Makes 10 servings.

Per 1 fajita serving	Cal	Fat	Sat. Fat	Chol	Sodium	Carbs	Fiber	Sugar	Protein
Something Better	**33**	**2g**	**0g**	**0mg**	**42mg**	**3g**	**0g**	**2g**	**0g**

menu

Tacos or Tostadas Menu

Taco or tostada shells

Taco Burger Crumbles

Refried Beans (page 79)

Melty Cheese (page 127) or soy cheddar cheese

Aioli (page 130) or commercial **soy sour cream**

Salsa (page 32) or commercial salsa

Guilt-Free Guacamole (page 126)

or commercial guacamole

Shredded lettuce

Diced tomatoes

Black olives

Taco Burger Crumbles

"Beef up" your tacos with a healthy homemade burger crumble full of fiber and all kinds of good stuff. If you don't have time to make your own, you can always buy vegetarian burger at the store!

2 cups **bulgur wheat**

2 cans (15 ounces) tomatoes, with juice

1 cup walnuts or sunflower seeds

1 small onion, chopped

½ cup Taco Seasoning (page 151) or commercial taco seasoning

4 cloves garlic

2 tablespoons molasses

2 teaspoons salt

1 Preheat oven to 275°F. Lightly coat a baking sheet with non-stick cooking spray.

2 Place bulgur wheat in a medium saucepan.

3 Combine remaining ingredients in a blender; blend until smooth and pour over bulgur. Place an additional ½ cup water in the blender; puree briefly to rinse out, and pour over bulgur mixture. Bring mixture to a boil over high heat; reduce to a simmer and cook 20 minutes, stirring often.

4 Spread mixture evenly on prepared baking sheet; bake 45 to 60 minutes, stirring occasionally, being careful not to overcook. Remove from oven while still a little moist. Makes 7 ½ cups.

Make it a Mix on page 151 →

 NOW & LATER:

This homemade taco burger freezes well! Make extra and keep it in your freezer for a quick meal. It's also great in chili.

 CHANGE IT UP:

Burger Crumbles: Leave out the taco seasoning and you have a great plain burger crumble to use in spaghetti sauce or sloppy joes.

 SHORTCUT:

Use vegetarian ground beef crumbles and commercial taco seasoning. Follow instructions on taco seasoning packet, using half of the water.

 CHANGE IT UP:

Make a chicken taco instead! Just use the Mexican Style Chicken (page 79) instead of the Taco Burger.

Per ⅓ cup serving	Cal	Fat	Sat. Fat	Chol	Sodium	Carbs	Fiber	Sugar	Protein
Traditional Recipe	116	6g	2g	33mg	312mg	2g	0g	0g	10g
Something Better	**94**	**3g**	**0g**	**0mg**	**423mg**	**15g**	**3g**	**3g**	**3g**

Mexican Style Chicken

Give your Veggie Fajita or Burrito a little something special with some Mexican Style Chicken. Save yourself a step and cook this with the Fajita Veggies (page 76) and you will have a real Mexican-style feast!

4 cups Gluten Steaks (page 48), cut in strips
Prepared **Soy Curls** (page 150), or other **chicken substitute** of your choice
1 tablespoon oil
2 tablespoons Taco Seasoning (page 151) or **1** tablespoon commercial taco seasoning

TO COOK IN THE OVEN

1 Preheat oven to 400°F.
2 Combine all ingredients and place on a large baking sheet coated with non-stick cooking spray.
3 Bake at 400° for 20 minutes, stirring twice. (This is a great method to use if you are already making the Roasted Fajita Veggies (page 76)).

TO COOK ON THE STOVE TOP

1 Combine all ingredients in a large skillet over medium heat.
2 Cook until browned on all sides, adding a little water if needed to prevent sticking.
Makes 12 servings.

TIP:

If you are using a commercial brand of taco seasoning mix, you won't need to use as much of it— it's a bit spicier than our homemade kind.

Refried Beans

My friend Sara, who grew up in Mexico, taught me to make these great homemade refried beans. They are so good, I can eat them by the bowlful!

2 cups dry beans (pinto, black, red, pink, cranberry, or combination)
½ medium onion, chopped
½ teaspoon garlic, minced (optional)
1 tablespoon oil
1 teaspoon salt

1 Soak and cook beans until tender, following the instructions on page 149, adding onion and garlic before cooking.
2 Using a slotted spoon, scoop beans into a food processor or blender, reserving some of the water. Add oil and salt to blender; blend mixture until smooth, using reserved water as needed to achieve desired consistency. Depending on the size of your blender, you may need to blend the beans in two batches.
Makes 12 servings.

TIP:

Make beans a little thinner than you like because they will thicken as they sit.

Per ½ cup serving	Cal	Fat	Sat. Fat	Chol	Sodium	Carbs	Fiber	Sugar	Protein
Something Better	124	1g	0g	0mg	161mg	21g	5g	0g	7g

Black Beans

My son likes to get the black beans in his burrito if we go to our favorite Mexican restaurant. It got me thinking beyond using only refried beans for burritos. I am glad he had this idea!

5 cups cold water, more as needed

1 ½ cups dried black beans

1 medium onion, chopped

½ medium green bell pepper, chopped

2 ½ tablespoons **Chicken Style Seasoning** (page 152) or commercial chicken seasoning

2 teaspoons ground cumin

2 teaspoons garlic, minced

2 bay leaves

2 teaspoons dried oregano

1 teaspoon salt

1 can (15 ounces) diced tomatoes

1 tablespoon lemon juice

1 Soak and cook beans according to the instructions on page 149.

2 Add onion, bell pepper, chicken seasoning, cumin, garlic, bay leaves, oregano, and salt to beans about half way through cooking time. Add additional water as needed.

3 Add tomatoes and lemon juice when beans are soft and heated through. Discard bay leaves before serving.

Makes 6 servings.

NOW & LATER:

Plan for leftovers and make a great Black Bean and Rice Casserole by layering rice and beans in a 9-by-13-inch pan and bake at 350°F until hot. Cover with Aioli (page 130) or commercial **soy sour cream** and sprinkle with diced tomatoes and green onions.

SHORTCUT:

Prefer to use canned beans? Sauté the onion and pepper in a large saucepan until soft. Add 2 (15 ounce) cans of black beans, 3 cups of water, and the seasonings. Simmer for 30 minutes. Add tomatoes and lemon juice; heat through. Discard bay leaves before serving.

CHANGE IT UP:

Black Beans and Rice: Serve over Flaky Brown Rice (page 123) with Tomato, Cucumber, Tomato and Avocado Salad (page 32), Aioli (page 130), or commercial **soy sour cream** and green onions.

TIP:

The acid in tomatoes prevents beans from softening, so make sure you always add them at the end of the cooking time!

Per ½ cup serving	Cal	Fat	Sat. Fat	Chol	Sodium	Carbs	Fiber	Sugar	Protein
Something Better	104	0g	0g	0mg	212mg	20g	5g	1g	6g

menu

General Chow's Tofu

The secret to great Chinese food at home is the sauce! The sauce on this General Chow's Tofu is perfect—far better than some of those bottle sauces at the grocery store.

SAUCE

1 tablespoon oil

¼ cup onion, minced

2 tablespoons garlic, minced

2 teaspoons ginger, minced

1 ⅓ cups vegetable broth

¼ cup **Braggs Liquid Aminos** or low sodium soy sauce

⅓ cup sugar

2 tablespoons lemon juice

dash cayenne pepper, or to taste

2 tablespoons water

2 tablespoons cornstarch

TOFU

1 package (14 ounces) water-packed **tofu**, firm or extra-firm

¾ cup cornstarch

oil, as needed for frying

FINISH IT OFF

1 bunch broccoli

SAUCE

1 Heat oil in a medium skillet over medium heat.

2 Add onion, garlic, and ginger; cook about 4 minutes, until onions are softened.

3 Add vegetable broth, soy sauce, sugar, lemon juice, and cayenne pepper; bring to a boil.

4 Mix water with cornstarch in a small bowl; add to boiling sauce. Cook until thickened.

TOFU

1 Drain excess water from tofu. (See "How to" on page 150)

2 Cut tofu into ½-inch cubes and toss with the cornstarch until completely coated.

3 Cover bottom of skillet with a generous layer of oil over medium heat.

4 Add tofu to skillet; fry until browned. Turn tofu and brown the other side. Remove from pan.

5 Add broccoli to hot pan with a couple of tablespoons of water; cook until crisp-tender.

6 Add tofu and sauce back to pan; mix well before serving.

Makes 6 servings.

 TIP:

This sauce is great for dipping Spring Rolls (page 125).

 SHORTCUT:

Use instant brown rice.

TIP:

Out of vegetable broth? Make your own broth using this easy formula: 1 tablespoon **Chicken Style Seasoning** (page 152) to 1 cup of water.

Per serving	Cal	Fat	Sat. Fat	Chol	Sodium	Carbs	Fi
General Tso's Chicken	479	31g	4g	62mg	695mg	35g	1
Something Better	**339**	**3g**	**0g**	**0mg**	**512mg**	**40g**	4

menu

Dominican Beans

It took some coaxing, but I was able to get this recipe from a friend of mine from the Dominican Republic. She had never actually measured anything for the dish in all her years of cooking it, so in the process of putting it on paper for me, it was her first time getting the "recipe" too! It is definitely a recipe worth keeping.

4 cups dried pinto beans
¾ large onion, cut into 3 large pieces
¾ medium red or green bell pepper, seeds removed, cut into 3 large pieces
1 ½ tablespoons salt
1 can (8 ounces) tomato sauce
1 handful fresh cilantro, approximately ¼ cup loosely packed

1 Soak beans in water overnight.

2 In the morning, discard soaking water and add enough fresh water to cover beans by 3 inches.

3 Bring to a boil over high heat; cook over medium-low about 45 to 60 minutes, until beans are almost done. (Be sure to keep enough water in your beans and stir occasionally to avoid burning.)

4 Add onion, bell pepper, and salt to the pot. Simmer 45 to 60 minutes, until beans are cooked and vegetables are soft. Keep beans covered with 2 inches of water, adding additional water if needed.

5 Remove all onion and pepper pieces from the beans with a slotted spoon; place in a blender with 1 cup of beans and enough "bean water" to blend.

6 Add tomato sauce and cilantro to blender and blend until smooth. Pour mixture back into the beans and stir to mix well.

Makes 10 servings

 TIP:

This is a great recipe to go with Spanish Rice (page 124). They use a lot of the same ingredients and taste great together.

 NOW & LATER:

These beans are great in Burritos (page 70 & 74) or Haystacks (page 111), and they freeze well.

 SHORTCUT:

Use the Crockpot method for cooking beans on page 149. Place soaked beans, onions and peppers in the Crockpot in the morning and cook for a minimum of 8 hours. Then proceed with remainder of recipe from step 5.

Per ¾ cup serving	Cal	Fat	Sat. Fat	Chol	Sodium	Carbs	Fiber	Sugar	Protein
Something Better	**281**	**1g**	**0g**	**0mg**	**985mg**	**51g**	**13g**	**3g**	**17g**

menu

Dhal

Coconut Rice (page 123)

or Flaky Brown Rice (page 123)

Cucumber slices

Steamed cauliflower

Dhal (Indian Lentils)

It's great to give your family a chance to try food from different cultures.
This Indian Dhal is a simple recipe to try for a taste of India.

2 tablespoons oil
½ medium onion, chopped
2 teaspoons, rounded , garlic paste
2 teaspoons, rounded, fresh grated gingerroot or ginger paste
1 can (6 ounces) tomato paste
2 teaspoons, rounded, mild curry paste
1 teaspoon ground coriander
1 teaspoon ground cumin
4 cups water
1 can (14 ounces) lite coconut milk
1 cup dried red lentils
¼ teaspoon salt, or to taste

1 Heat oil in large saucepan over medium heat. Add onion; cook until softened, stirring occasionally.

2 Add garlic and ginger; cook 1 minute, stirring.

3 Add tomato paste, curry paste, coriander, and cumin; cook 3 minutes, stirring constantly to avoid burning.

4 Add water, coconut milk, and lentils; stir to mix well.

5 Bring to a boil over high heat; reduce to a simmer and cook, partially covered, until lentils are soft, 40 to 45 minutes, stirring occasionally and adding water as needed. Season with salt and serve.

Makes 6 servings.

Per 1 cup serving	Cal	Fat	Sat. Fat	Chol	Sodium	Carbs	Fiber	Sugar	Protein
Something Better	**257**	**11g**	**5g**	**0mg**	**227mg**	**32g**	**6g**	**7g**	**12g**

menu

Szechwan Style Chicken

Flaky Brown Rice (page 123)

or instant brown rice

Asian Salad (page 26)

Szechwan-Style Chicken

Have you ever wanted to make Chinese food at home? Now you can! Here is a great restaurant-style dish that your family will love. Our Szechwan sauce is not as spicy as the original, but you can kick it up a bit if you want.

SZECHWAN SAUCE

2 ¼ cups water

¼ cup tomato paste

3 tablespoons cornstarch

2 tablespoons lemon juice

1 tablespoon **Braggs Liquid Aminos** or low sodium soy sauce

4 teaspoons **cane juice crystals** or sugar

2 teaspoons **Chicken Style Seasoning** (page 152) or commercial chicken seasoning

1 (½-inch) slice ginger, peeled and smashed

¼ to ½ teaspoon cayenne pepper (optional)

ALL THE REST

1 tablespoon oil

3 cups **prepared Soy Curls** (page 150) or other **chicken substitute**

2 (½-inch) slices ginger, smashed

2 cups sugar snap peas

1 can (8 ounces) water chestnuts, drained and chopped

1 tablespoon toasted sesame oil (optional)

1 bunch green onions, minced

½ cup dry-roasted peanuts or cashews

1 recipe Flaky Brown rice (page 123)

SZECHUAN SAUCE

1 Whisk all sauce ingredients together in a medium bowl; set aside.

ALL THE REST

1 Heat oil in a large non-stick skillet over medium. Add prepared Soy Curls and ginger; stir well.

2 Add sugar snap peas and water chestnuts; cook 4 minutes, stirring occasionally. Add a few tablespoons of water to skillet to prevent burning, if needed.

3 Stir in reserved sauce; cook 3 to 4 minutes, until thickened.

4 Remove from heat; discard ginger and add sesame oil.

5 Sprinkle with green onions and nuts to garnish.

Makes 6 servings.

NOW & LATER:

Make the sauce ahead of time. It will keep in the refrigerator for up to one week.

SHORTCUT:

Use a commercial **chicken substitute**, such as Morning Star Farms Meal Starters or Lightlife Chick'n Strips, and instant brown rice.

Per ¾ cup serving	Cal	Fat	Sat. Fat	Chol	Sodium	Carbs	Fiber	Sugar	Protein
Traditional Recipe	560	10g	3g	160mg	2595mg	45g	8g	0g	61g
Something Better	**260**	**16g**	**2g**	**0mg**	**191mg**	**21g**	**5g**	**7g**	**10g**

menu

Pancit (Filipino Noodles)

NOODLES

1 package (6 ounces) rice sticks or rice noodles

2 tablespoons **Chicken Style Seasoning** (page 152) or commercial chicken seasoning

¼ teaspoon ground turmeric

ALL THE REST

1 package (14 ounces) water-packed **tofu**, firm or extra-firm, cut into ½-inch cubes

2 tablespoons oil, divided

3 to 4 tablespoons **Bragg's Liquid Aminos** or low sodium soy sauce, to taste, divided

1 large onion, sliced into crescents

5 cloves garlic, minced

3 cups cabbage, shredded

1 ½ cups carrots, julienned

1 ½ cups celery, julienned

1 ½ cups broccoli or pea pods

5 green onions, finely chopped

4 cups vegetable broth or broth made with **Chicken Style Seasoning** (page 169)

1 tablespoon vegetarian mushroom seasoning or **beef style seasoning**

½ tablespoon cornstarch

1 teaspoon salt

In the Philippines, everybody has their own Pancit recipe, so we took ideas from our Filipino friends and made one of our own. Don't be intimidated by the long list of ingredients. They are almost all vegetables, and if you are not into all that chopping, check out the shortcut. It works like a charm to get this dinner on the table in a hurry!

1 Soak rice noodles in a bowl of very hot water to cover, according to the package directions.

2 Meanwhile, bring a large pot of water to a boil. Add soaked rice noodles and remaining noodles ingredients; cook 3 minutes. Drain noodles, cut to desired length, and set aside.

3 Drain excess water from tofu. (See "How To" on page 150)

4 Heat 1 tablespoon oil in a large non-stick skillet over medium; add tofu and 1 to 2 tablespoons soy sauce. Cook until browned on all sides; remove from pan and set aside.

5 Add onion and garlic to skillet with remaining 1 tablespoon oil; cook until just softened, about 2 minutes.

6 Add cabbage, carrots, and celery to skillet; cook 4 to 5 minutes, stirring occasionally.

7 Add broccoli or snow peas and green onions; cook until just tender.

8 Add reserved rice noodles and tofu to skillet; stir well.

9 Mix together remaining ingredients and 2 tablespoons soy sauce in a medium bowl; add to skillet and cook 3 to 5 minutes.

Makes 6 servings.

TIP:

The longer you cook the tofu, the more chewy and less mushy it will become, so cook it until you are happy with the texture.

SHORTCUT:

Use 1 bag of Broccoli Slaw or Rainbow Slaw mix and 1 bag of Cole Slaw mix in place of all of the veggies.

Per 1 cup serving	Cal	Fat	Sat. Fat	Chol	Sodium	Carbs	Fiber	Sugar	Protein
Traditional Recipe	304	11g	3g	58mg	698mg	27g	4g	6g	24g
Something Better	**295**	**10g**	**1g**	**0mg**	**1024mg**	**42g**	**6g**	**7g**	**12g**

menu

Mac & Cheese

Steamed broccoli

Raw veggies and Ranch Dressing

(page 34), for dipping

Mac & Cheese

I have tried this recipe out on kids from Alabama to Michigan and every one of them loved it!

1 box (14 ounces) whole wheat macaroni noodles, cooked according to package directions

4 cups water, divided

1 cup **raw cashews**

½ cup oil

½ cup pimento peppers or bottled roasted red peppers

¼ cup **nutritional yeast flakes**

3 ½ tablespoons lemon juice

½ tablespoon salt

2 teaspoons onion powder

½ teaspoon garlic powder

1 Preheat oven to 350°F. Lightly coat a 9-by-13-inch baking dish with non-stick cooking spray.

2 Blend 2 cups water and nuts in a blender until very smooth and creamy. This can take several minutes, depending on your blender. (See "How To" on page 150 for instructions)

3 Add remaining ingredients, except pasta, to blender; blend until smooth and creamy.

4 Combine blended mixture and pasta in prepared baking dish; stir well to mix.

5 Bake 45 minutes.

Makes 12 servings.

NOW & LATER:

American Cheeze Sauce (page 127) works great in this recipe, too, and you can make a double batch to use in Cheezie Potatoes (page 119) or any of the Mexican recipes.

SHORTCUT:

If you want to save time, add ¼ cup cornstarch to the blended mixture and thicken the sauce over the stove. Mix it into the cooked noodles and serve immediately instead of baking it.

Per ¾ cup serving	Cal	Fat	Sat. Fat	Chol	Sodium	Carbs	Fiber	Sugar	Protein
Traditional Recipe	290	9g	5g	20mg	560mg	41g	2g	2g	11g
Something Better	**231**	**15g**	**2g**	**0mg**	**290mg**	**19g**	**2g**	**2g**	**6g**

menu

Veggie Subs

Veggie Subs

Mom's Potato Salad (page 29)

Chips

Carrot and celery sticks

Veggie Subs

Our family loves going out to eat subs but they can be kind of expensive with my big eaters, so we decided to make our own at home.

8 whole-grain sub buns
Soy cheese slices (optional)
Aioli (page 130) or
commercial **soy mayonnaise**
Vegetarian soy meat
slices, such as Tofurky,
Smart Deli, Yves, etc.
Green peppers, sliced
Sweet onions, sliced
Tomatoes, sliced
Lettuce, shredded
Carrots, shredded (optional)
Olives, sliced (optional)
Cucumbers, sliced (optional)
Favorite Italian Dressing
(page 34, variation)

1 Preheat oven to 350°F. Place cheese on sub buns and toast under broiler until lightly browned. Spread with mayonnaise.

2 Place 2 or 3 slices of veggie meat on each sub bun and top with desired veggies.

3 Drizzle 1 tablespoon of Favorite Italian Dressing over the veggies.

Makes 8 subs.

TIP:

If you have a food processor, use the slicing blade attachment instead of prepping veggies with a knife. you can make quick work of all the slicing.

TIP:

Believe it or not, the key to a great tasting sub is the shredded lettuce. It helps to hold the dressing and keep the flavor.

Per 1 sandwich serving	Cal	Fat	Sat. Fat	Chol	Sodium	Carbs	Fiber	Sugar	Protein
Something Better	336	17g	1g	0mg	276mg	29g	6g	5g	15g

menu

Bar-B-Que Chicken Sandwich

Coleslaw (page 28)

Sweet Potato Fries (page 122)

Bar-B-Q Chicken Sandwich

Growing up in Missouri, we were always up for a good barbeque. Now that I am a vegetarian, I still need my barbeque every once in a while, and this sandwich really hits the spot!

BAR-B-Q SAUCE

⅔ cup lemon juice

½ cup water

½ cup brown sugar

1 can (6 ounces) tomato paste

2 tablespoons **non-hydrogenated margarine**

2 teaspoons chili powder

1 teaspoon liquid smoke

1 teaspoon molasses

½ teaspoon salt

FINISH IT OFF

1 tablespoon oil

3 cups prepared **Soy Curls** (page 150) or other **chicken substitute** (page 153)

½ medium onion, sliced (optional)

½ medium pepper, green or red, sliced (optional)

6 whole grain buns, toasted if desired

1 Mix Bar-B-Q Sauce ingredients together in a medium saucepan; bring to a boil over high heat. Reduce to a simmer and cook until thickened and slightly reduced, about 30 minutes.

2 Heat oil in a large saucepan over medium; add onions and peppers. Cook until softened; add prepared Soy Curls and mix well.

3 Pour reserved Bar-B-Q sauce over Soy Curls mixture; cook until thick and bubbly, about 10 minutes.

4 Serve on a toasted bun.

Makes 6 servings.

SHORTCUT:

Use a bottled Bar-B-Q sauce. Just make sure to read your labels carefully—they are usually full of high-fructose corn syrup and other questionable ingredients.

CHANGE IT UP:

Sloppy Joes: Just use Burger Crumbles, if you have them in the freezer (page 78, variation), or a commercial brand in place of the **Soy Curls**.

TIP:

If you don't have **Soy Curls** prepared you can just soak them and add them to the pan with peppers and onions with the Soy Curls seasonings.

Per ½ cup serving	Cal	Fat	Sat. Fat	Chol	Sodium	Carbs	Fiber	Sugar	Protein
Traditional Recipe	516	17g	4g	94mg	887mg	36g	3g	7g	32g
Something Better	**343**	**9g**	**2g**	**0mg**	**477mg**	**56g**	**8g**	**30g**	**13g**

menu

Better Burgers

Lettuce, tomato, onion, or desired toppings

Steak Fries (page 121)

Broccoli Salad (page 27)

TEX-MEX BURGER

Guilt-Free Guacamole (page 126)

or sliced avocado

Veggie bacon strips or Baco Bits

Lettuce, onions, and tomato slices

Aioli (page 130)

or commercial **soy mayonnaise**

SPECIAL SAUCE BURGER

Thousand Island Dressing (page 33)

Pickles

Lettuce, onions, and tomato slices

Soy American cheese slices

BBQ BURGER

BBQ Sauce (page 96)

or commercial brand

Caramelized onion

Lettuce, tomatoes, and mayo

MUSHROOM SWISS BURGER

Sautéed mushrooms and onions

Soy Swiss cheese slices

Better Burgers

Vegetarian burgers are easy to come by these days. Most restaurants have their version and you can buy them at your local grocery store. This healthy version tastes great and can be made for a fraction of the cost.

2 cups quick-cooking oats

¼ to ½ cup walnuts, finely chopped

⅓ cup **whole wheat flour**

1 can (15 ounces) garbanzo beans, undrained

¾ cup water

1 medium onion, quartered

2 tablespoons **Bragg's Liquid Aminos** or low sodium soy sauce

1 teaspoon salt

1 teaspoon dried sage

16 whole grain hamburger buns

1 Preheat oven to 350°F.

2 Mix together oats, walnuts, and flour in a large bowl; set aside.

3 Combine remaining ingredients, except buns, in a blender; blend until smooth.

4 Pour blended mixture into oat mixture; stir to combine.

5 Let sit 10 minutes to absorb moisture.

6 Use an ice cream scoop or ¼-cup measuring cup to make 16 burgers; flatten each to ½-inch thick and place on a baking sheet.

7 Bake 45 minutes, turning once after 25 minutes.

Makes 16 patties.

SHORTCUT:

Check the freezer section of your grocery store for frozen veggie burgers. Using them makes this a quick and easy meal.

Per 1 patty serving	Cal	Fat	Sat. Fat	Chol	Sodium	Carbs	Fiber	Sugar	Protein
Traditional Recipe	540	29g	10g	75mg	1040mg	45g	3g	9g	50g
Something Better	**267**	**5g**	**0g**	**0mg**	**669g**	**45g**	**8g**	**4g**	**12g**

menu

Pizza (see page 100)

All American Salad (page 26)

Per 2 piece serving	Cal	Fat	Sat. Fat	Chol	Sodium	Carbs	Fiber	Sugar	Protein
Something Better	292	5g	0g	0mg	358mg	54g	8g	5g	11g

Pizza crust

Make your pizza "better" with whole grain crust and well- chosen toppings. We have given you several options on the next page; don't be afraid to try something new!

1 ½ cups + 2 tablespoons warm water (13 ounces)

2 tablespoons oil

1 ½ teaspoons salt

2 tablespoons honey

2 cups + 2 tablespoons **whole wheat flour** (we like white whole wheat)

2 cups unbleached flour

2 tablespoons vital wheat gluten

1 ½ teaspoons instant yeast

HAND METHOD

1 Combine all ingredients in a large mixing bowl; mix with a spoon.

2 Once combined, knead dough on a lightly floured surface, adding as little flour as possible, until dough is smooth and elastic, about 7 to 10 minutes total.

3 Place dough in a warm, draft-free place; cover with a damp towel. Allow dough to rise until doubled in size, about 1 hour.

BREAD MACHINE METHOD

Place all ingredients in a bread machine in the order listed. Select the "dough" setting and press "start."

ROLLING THE DOUGH

Divide dough into 2 equal pieces. Place on parchment paper and roll out to the desired thickness and transfer to pan.

BAKING THE PIZZA

1 Par bake dough for 7 minutes in a preheated 350°F oven.

2 Add Tomato Sauce (page 67) or Basil Pesto (page 129) and desired toppings.

3 Bake an additional 10 minutes, or until crust is golden brown.

FOR THE BEST CRUST EVER

1 Place baking stone in a 500°F oven, preheat about 1 hour.

2 Roll dough out on parchment paper, as described above. Add desired toppings. Keeping dough on paper, transfer to hot stone in oven.

3 Reduce heat to 450°F; bake 8 to 10 minutes.

Makes 8 servings or two 14-inch pizzas.

SHORTCUT:
Buy frozen whole wheat bread dough to make your own whole wheat pizza crust. You can also buy premade whole grain pizza crusts at most grocery stores.

 TIP:
You can freeze your par baked crusts and save them for another day!

PESTO PIZZA

Basil Pesto (page 129)

Onions

Green peppers

Black olives

Diced tomatoes

Banana peppers

Fake Feta (page 129)

or Soy mozzarella cheese

SUPREME PIZZA

Tomato Sauce (page 67)

Sausage crumbles

Veggie pepperoni

Onions

Green peppers

Mushrooms

Black olives

Soy mozzarella cheese

VEGGIE LOVERS PIZZA

Veggie Lovers Pizza

Tomato Sauce (page 67)

Onions

Green peppers

Black olives

Spinach

Tomatoes

Artichoke hearts

Melty Cheeze (page 127)

GREEK PIZZA

Olive oil & fresh minced garlic

for sauce

Nondairy parmesan cheese

Black olives

Diced tomatoes

Green peppers

Red onions

Fake Feta (page 129)

Fresh basil leaves

Garlic Feta Dressing (page 33)

drizzled on top

Basic Pizza

Pizza Crust (page 100)
or frozen whole wheat bread dough
Tomato Sauce (page 67)
Toppings of your choice

Bake according to the directions for your desired crust.

 SHORTCUT:
Use commercial pizza crust
and sauce.

BAR-B-Q CHICKEN PIZZA

Bar-B-Q Chicken (page 96)

Red onions

Soy mozzarella cheese

TRADITIONAL PIZZA

Tomato Sauce (page 67)

Soy mozzarella cheese

Soy provolone cheese

Veggie pepperoni

HAWAIIAN PIZZA

Tomato Sauce (page 67)

Soy mozzarella cheese

Pineapple

Green pepper

Diced tomatoes

Sliced almonds

TUSCAN PIZZA

Basil Pesto (page 129)
for Sauce

Artichoke hearts

Sun-dried tomatoes

Diced tomatoes

Spinach

Fake Feta (page 129)

STOP & SMELL
the roses

The old saying "stop and smell the roses" seems to have originated from an old story of a lady who worked hard to make her rose garden beautiful. She weeded, she pruned, she cultivated. Every time she walked into her garden, she saw a poor stunted rose bush or an unsightly shrub, all needing her attention. It wasn't until a friend visited and told her to "stop and smell the roses" that she stepped back to look at the whole garden and was awestruck by the beauty of the flowers. Do you ever find yourself spending more time taking care of your family than you do actually enjoying them?

In all of the Blue Zones, family and community play an important role in health and longevity. The American Blue Zone, however, is unique in that they reserve an entire 24-hour period each week for building strong relationships with one another and with God. This period, the Sabbath (meaning rest), is taken directly from the creation week where God Himself rested from His work on the seventh day. Hence their name, Seventh-day Adventist, because they also rest on the seventh day.

The Adventists make the Sabbath a priority. No matter how busy or stressed they are, they stop for the Sabbath. In fact, they don't want to miss a single minute of this special time. So they prepare to enjoy a day of rest by making sure all work is completed before sundown on Friday, including food preparation, house cleaning, and putting away all differences and quarrels from the week. Freed from the worries and cares of life, they have time to build close connections with God as well as with family and friends. These connections are an important part of Blue Zone living, because they relieve stress and allow the brain to relax and rejuvenate.

Nobody ever looks back at their life saying "I wish I had spent more time at work or had kept my house cleaner." When you reflect on your priorities, I am sure you will agree that your relationships are the most important. Make a choice for "something better"—stop and "smell the roses" with your family and with God.

meals to share

The more the merrier!

Inviting family and friends over to build those lasting relationships sounds stressful but it doesn't have to be it all comes down to proper planning. In the previous pages of this book, you've probably noticed the "Now & Later Tips" included with some of the recipes. This section of our book will teach you how to put those leftovers to good use and make "something better" for your family and your guests, without a lot of stress!

"A happy heart is like good medicine, but a broken spirit drains your strength."

Proverbs 17:22, NCV

Tater Tot Casserole or Shepherd's Pie

This quick and easy crowd pleaser is great for a potluck with friends. And it is so easy to make, especially if you planned ahead with the Now & Later tips earlier in the week.

8 cups frozen mixed vegetables, thawed

4 cups Gluten Steaks (page 48), chopped into small pieces, or vegetarian burger crumbles

1 recipe Mushroom Gravy (page 128) or Brown Gravy (page 128)

Salt, to taste

1 bag tater tots, frozen or

4 cups mashed potatoes

1 Preheat oven to 350°F.

2 Mix vegetables, Gluten Steaks, and gravy in a large bowl. Add salt to taste.

3 Spread mixture into a 9-by-13-inch baking dish.

4 Cover with mashed potatoes or tater tots.

5 Bake 45 minutes, or until bubbly.

POTLUCK VERSION

Cook in a preheated 250°F oven 1 ½ to 2 hours. Increase the heat to 450°F for 10 minutes before serving to crisp the tater tots.

Makes 12 large servings.

 TIP:

If you are taking this to a potluck, add the tater tots just before you put it in the oven.

 SHORTCUT

If you don't have any Gluten Steaks in the freezer or didn't have them earlier in the week, you can use any commercial **beef substitute** (page 153) such as Morning Star Farms, Boca, or Lightlife.

 TIP:

The potluck version is great if you are taking it to church potluck. You can turn the heat up after the service while everyone is visiting and the other things are being put on the table. Your casserole will be done right on time!

Per 1 cup serving	Cal	Fat	Sat. Fat	Chol	Sodium	Carbs	Fiber	Sugar	Protein
Traditional Recipe	535	28g	11g	85mg	930mg	38g	3g	1g	32g
Something Better	**502**	**12g**	**2g**	**0mg**	**914mg**	**69g**	**15g**	**0g**	**35g**

Mexican Lasagna

Everybody enjoys Mexican food, so you can't go wrong serving this Mexican Lasagna to a crowd. This great casserole takes all the best parts of Mexican food and puts them into a one-dish meal, so it's easy to take with you or carry to a friend.

SAUCE

2 cans (15 ounces) diced tomatoes

1 can (16 ounces) tomato sauce

1 ½ cups Salsa (page 32) or commercial brand

1 tablespoon ground cumin

LASAGNA

12 whole grain lasagna noodles, cooked according to package directions, or corn tortillas

2 cups corn, canned or frozen

2 cans (15 ounces) black beans, drained and rinsed, or

4 cups Refried Beans (page 79) or Haystack Beans (page 112)

2 cups Melty Cheeze (page 127) or soy cheddar cheese

½ cup green onions, sliced

1 Preheat oven to 450°F. Coat a 9-by-13-inch baking dish with non-stick cooking spray.

2 Combine sauce ingredients together in a medium bowl.

3 Spread 1 ⅓ cups of sauce mixture along bottom of prepared dish.

4 Arrange 4 noodles over sauce.

5 Top with 1 cup corn, half of the beans, and a layer of cheese.

6 Repeat layers once; top with remaining 4 noodles.

7 Spread remaining sauce over noodles; top with remaining cheese.

8 Cover and bake 30 to 40 minutes, until sauce is bubbly.

9 Let stand 15 minutes before serving. Sprinkle with green onions and serve.

Makes 16 servings.

TIP:

Make it wheat free by using corn tortillas in place of the lasagna noodles.

TIP:

Bring some extra salsa and Aioli (page 130) or commercial **soy sour cream** to serve with this wonderful casserole.

TIP:

If you are going to a potluck that is short on oven space, you can heat this up at home before you leave. Wrap it in a thick layer of newspaper and towel and it will keep warm for hours. Or you can buy one of those great carry-along insulated pans that keeps things warm.

Per 2 piece serving	Cal	Fat	Sat. Fat	Chol	Sodium	Carbs	Fiber	Sugar	Protein
Something Better	**228**	**2g**	**0g**	**0mg**	**593mg**	**44g**	**5g**	**5g**	**9g**

Pasta Bar

When inviting people over, it is nice to serve a meal with all the elements separate so everyone can eat what they like and leave out what they don't. Since pasta is a favorite with young and old, everybody can find something they like with this meal.

1 recipe Tomato Sauce (page 67) or
2 jars of commercial spaghetti sauce
1 recipe Alfredo Sauce (page 68)
1 recipe Basil Pesto (page 129)
1 recipe Pecan Meatballs (page 58)
2 pounds cooked pasta, various noodles (such as spaghetti and shells)
8 cups steamed vegetables (such as carrots, cauliflower, and broccoli) or
2 bags of "California Blend" frozen vegetables
nondairy parmesan cheese
3 tomatoes, diced or grape tomatoes, sliced
Italian Salad (page 25)
Garlic Bread (See TIP page 60)

Makes 8 to 10 servings.

TIP:

Go a little crazy and get some fun shaped pasta; the kids will love it!

NOW & LATER:

It's later! If you planned ahead during the week, most of the work is already done!

TIP:

If you are serving an extra-large crowd, ask each family to bring one item for the Pasta Bar.

Haystacks

Corn chips or Tortilla Chips
1 recipe Haystack Beans, (page 112),
Dominican Beans (page 84), or
Black Beans (page 80)
1 recipe Flaky Brown Rice (page 123)
1 recipe Melty Cheeze (page 127) or
soy cheese
1 head lettuce, shredded
3 tomatoes, diced
1 can black olives, sliced
½ onion, diced
1 recipe Salsa (page 32) or
1 jar commercial salsa
1 recipe Aioli (page 130) or
commercial **soy sour cream**
1 recipe Guilt-Free
Guacamole (page 126)
1 recipe Ranch Dressing (page 34)

An all-around Adventist favorite! It is really a make-your-own taco salad—great for sharing because everyone gets to pick and choose the things they like as they build it. But be careful and start small—a Haystack can grow very quickly!

This is a basic guideline for serving Haystacks for 8 to 10 people. These are only guidelines—you can choose to use as many or few toppings as you like.

Haystack Beans

4 cups dried beans
(such as pinto, black, or red)
1 large onion, chopped
½ medium green bell pepper, chopped
½ cup Taco Seasoning Mix (page 151) or
1 envelope commercial taco seasoning
1 can (28 ounces) crushed tomatoes
1 tablespoon salt

1 Rinse and soak beans according to instructions on page 149.

2 Add onion, bell pepper, and Taco Seasoning to soaked beans.

3 Cook beans according to page 149, using either the Crockpot method or the stove top method.

4 When beans are tender, add tomatoes; simmer 30 minutes and serve.

Makes 16 servings.

 TIP:

Don't worry if you are running late for lunch, these beans can cook as long as you need them to, especially if you are using a Crockpot.

 TIP:

Most of the chopping can be done a day ahead in a food processor, except the lettuce. You will want to do that the same day.

 SHORTCUT:

Use canned chili beans or leftover Dominican Beans (page 84)

TIP:

No time to cook your own beans? Sauté onions and peppers until tender. Add Taco Seasoning and 3 large cans of pinto beans. Simmer to blend the flavors.

Per ½ cup serving	Cal	Fat	Sat. Fat	Chol	Sodium	Carbs	Fiber	Sugar	Protein
Something Better	**192**	**0g**	**0g**	**0mg**	**171mg**	**36g**	**9g**	**2g**	**11g**

Potato Bar

Perfect for a get-together with people of different tastes. I mean, who doesn't like potatoes! The toppings are so versatile that everyone can find something they like. And on the off-chance somebody doesn't like potatoes…the toppings are good without them!

18 baked potatoes
1 recipe Haystack Beans (page 112) or your favorite chili
1 recipe American Cheeze Sauce (page 127) or Melty Cheese (page 127)
2 heads broccoli, steamed
1 recipe Aioli (page 130) or commercial **soy sour cream**
1 jar Baco Bits
1 bunch green onions
1 recipe Salsa (page 32) or
1 jar commercial salsa
Seven-Layer Salad (page 30)

Serve buffet style, allowing guests to choose the toppings they like best!
Makes 8 to 10 servings.

SHORTCUT:
Use canned chili beans or leftover Dominican Beans (page 84).

TIP:
Keep beans hot by using a Crockpot.

Per serving	Cal	Fat	Sat. Fat	Chol	Sodium	Carbs	Fiber	Sugar	Protein
Something Better	228	2g	0g	0mg	593mg	44g	5g	5g	9g

ADDING YEARS TO
your life

"Living until 90 is not as hard as you might think.
Even at 70, it's possible to make a difference in your health."

——Archives of Internal Medicine. Feb 11, 2008

+2 years	Be a vegetarian
+2 years	Eat a handful of nuts everyday
+10 years	Don't smoke
+4 years	Exercise regularly
+3 to 4 years	Maintain a healthy body weight
+7 years	Volunteer once a week
+7 to 14 years	Attend church

+35 to 43 years!

Doll, Richard; et al. (26 June 2004). "Mortality in relation to smoking: 50 years' observations on male British doctors." British Medical Journal 328 (7455): 1519
Fraser, Gary E. Diet, Life Expectancy, and Chronic Disease: Studies of Seventh-day Adventists and Other Vegetarians. Oxford University Press, 2003
Buettner, Dan,, The Blue Zones: Lessons fro Living Longer from the People Who've Lived the Longest. National Geographic, 2008.
http://www.cbsnews.com/stories/2009/11/14/earlyshow/saturday/main5645326.shtml

sides & sauces

Your partners in good health

The entrée may be the star of the meal, but side dishes bring it all together—they can really complete a meal by adding different colors, textures, and flavors to a plate. Healthy side dishes allow you to include more whole grains, fruits and vegetables into the meal, getting you one step closer to the "Strive for five, but eight is great" goal. Your side dishes will taste so good, you might forget to eat the entrée!

"Pleasant words are as a honeycomb, sweet to the mind and healing to the body."

Proverbs 16:24, Amplified Bible

Steaming Vegetables

We all know that vegetables are packed full of vitamins and minerals. Serving them steamed as a side dish is a great way to get your 5 to 8 servings. Steamed vegetables can be served plain, with a drizzling of sauce or sprinkled with kosher salt.

It doesn't matter if you're steaming broccoli or peas; all vegetables are steamed with the same method. Place a steamer basket with a shallow layer of vegetables in a pot with one inch of water, making sure the water does not touch the vegetables. Bring the water to a boil and cover the steam pot with a lid.

Each vegetable does need to be steamed for different amounts of time, however. Here is an easy-to-follow chart for how long to steam various varieties of vegetables. Start the timer when the water begins to boil.

VEGETABLE	STEAMING TIME
Artichokes	40 minutes
Asparagus, spears	3 to 6 minutes
Beets	30 to 35 minutes
Broccoli, florets	5 to 6 minutes
Brussels sprouts	7 to 11 minutes
Cabbage, cut in wedges	6 minutes
Carrots, cut ¼-inch thick	6 to 8 minutes
Cauliflower florets	4 to 6 minutes
Green beans	4 to 5 minutes
Kale or other leafy greens	4 to 5 minutes
Peas	2 minutes
Potatoes & sweet potatoes, diced	12 to 15 minutes
Potatoes & sweet potatoes	40 to 50 minutes
Winter squash, peeled, 2-inch pieces	15 to 20 minutes

Green Bean Casserole

Thanksgiving would just not be the same without the Green Bean Casserole. This one is better for you than the one Mom used to make, so why wait for Thanksgiving to make it?

4 cans (15 ounces) green beans or
6 cups fresh beans, stemmed and cut
1 recipe Mushroom Gravy (page 128)
2 cups French-fried onion rings

1 Preheat oven to 350°F.

2 Steam fresh green beans according to chart on page 117 until tender. If using canned green beans, skip this step.

3 Combine green beans and Mushroom Gravy in a casserole dish.

4 Bake 20 to 30 minutes, until hot and bubbly.

5 Remove from oven and cover with French-fried onions. Return to oven and cook 3 to 5 minutes, until onions are golden brown.

Makes 14 servings.

TIP:

Stir a few dollops of commercial **soy sour cream** in with the Mushroom Gravy for a little extra creaminess.

Per ½ cup serving	Cal	Fat	Sat. Fat	Chol	Sodium	Carbs	Fiber	Sugar	Protein
Traditional Recipe	110	8g	3g	0mg	460mg	8g	1g	2g	2g
Something Better	**103**	**6g**	**2g**	**0mg**	**429mg**	**9g**	**2g**	**0g**	**1g**

Cheezie Potatoes

Who says potatoes are not vegetables? They are one of the best sources of potassium and fiber in the produce section and they also have half of the recommended daily amount of vitamin C. These potatoes are creamy and cheesy—the perfect potato dish to compliment to any "almost meat and potatoes" meal.

5 medium white potatoes, thinly sliced

1 medium onion, diced

1 teaspoon salt, divided

2 ½ cups American Cheeze Sauce (page 127), not thickened

1 cup **nondairy milk,** unsweetened

1 Preheat oven to 350°F. Coat a 9-by-13-inch baking dish with non-stick cooking spray.

2 Layer half of the potatoes along the bottom of prepared dish; top with ¾ of the onion. Sprinkle with ½ teaspoon salt.

3 Mix Cheeze and milk together in a medium bowl; pour half of the Cheeze mixture over potatoes and onions.

4 Top with another layer of potatoes, onions, and Cheeze; sprinkle with ½ teaspoon salt.

5 Cover with aluminum foil; bake 1 hour and 15 minutes. Uncover and bake 15 minutes, until the top is golden brown.

Makes 16 servings.

 TIP:

If you have onion haters in your family, dice the onions small!

 TIP:

Use the thin slicing blade on your food processor to slice the potatoes

Per serving	Cal	Fat	Sat. Fat	Chol	Sodium	Carbs	Fiber	Sugar	Protein
Traditional Recipe	160	8g	1g	5mg	500mg	21g	2g	2g	2g
Something Better	**135**	**3g**	**0g**	**0mg**	**281mg**	**24g**	**3g**	**3g**	**4g**

Oven Roasted Potatoes

Roasting potatoes in the oven is great because it leaves you free to work on other things while they cook. Just make sure you set the timer in case you get caught up in another project. You don't want to set off the fire alarm!

5 medium red-skinned potatoes, washed and cut into bite-size cubes
2 tablespoons oil
2 cloves garlic, minced
2 ½ teaspoons salt
1 teaspoon onion powder

1 Preheat oven to 400°F. Coat a large baking sheet with non-stick cooking spray.
2 Steam potatoes until soft, or microwave on high 6 minutes.
3 Place potatoes in a large bowl; drizzle with oil and sprinkle with garlic, salt, and onion powder. Stir to coat.
4 Place potato mixture in a single layer on prepared baking sheet.
5 Bake 20 to 30 minutes, until potatoes are browned.

Makes 6 servings.

TIP:

Cut the potatoes the night before and they will be ready to bake when you get home from work. Be sure to keep them soaking in water to keep them from getting discolored.

CHANGE IT UP:

Roasted Garlic Potatoes: Add 2 more cloves of garlic and ½ teaspoon dried dill; serve with any of our "Almost Meat and Potatoes" meals.

CHANGE IT UP:

Replace some of the potatoes with carrots and onions. It's wonderful!

Per ¾ cup serving	Cal	Fat	Sat. Fat	Chol	Sodium	Carbs	Fiber	Sugar	Protein
Traditional Recipe	110	8g	3g	0mg	460mg	8g	1g	2g	2g
Something Better	**103**	**6g**	**2g**	**0mg**	**429mg**	**9g**	**2g**	**0g**	**1g**

Steak Fries

Big fat French fries…that is what steak fries are and, boy, are they good! The great thing is that they bake up nicely and you get to have control over the amount and type oil that you use.

4 large baking potatoes, peeled and cut into ¼-inch sticks

2 teaspoons oil

½ teaspoon onion powder

½ teaspoon garlic powder

¼ teaspoon salt

¼ to ½ teaspoon paprika

¼ teaspoon salt

1 Preheat oven to 350°F. Coat 2 baking sheets with non-stick cooking spray or line with parchment paper.

2 Blot potatoes with paper towels until dry.

3 Combine potatoes with remaining ingredients in a large bowl; toss to coat.

4 Spread potatoes in a single layer on prepared baking sheets. (If they are too crowded, the fries won't crisp up.)

5 Bake until fries are tender, turning occasionally, about 30 minutes.

6 Increase heat to 475°F; bake 5 to 8 minutes, until crispy and browned.

Makes 4 servings.

TIP:
For crisper fries, bake on a baking sheet with holes so that the air can circulate all around the fries.

TIP:
Using the parchment paper keeps your baking sheets clean.

 CHANGE IT UP:
Use a mix of white potatoes and sweet potatoes.

Per serving	Cal	Fat	Sat. Fat	Chol	Sodium	Carbs	Fiber	Sugar	Protein
Traditional Recipe	230	11g	2g	0mg	160mg	29g	3g	0g	3g
Something Better	**210**	**3g**	**0g**	**0mg**	**256mg**	**43g**	**5g**	**3g**	**5g**

Sweet Potato Fries

What better way to get nutrition than in the ever popular French fry? Sweet potatoes have so much nutrition that it's difficult to describe because you just don't know where to start—so change things up a bit and use sweet potatoes to make your fries.

5 medium sweet potatoes, peeled and cut into ¼-inch sticks

1 ½ tablespoons oil

2 ½ teaspoons salt

½ teaspoon paprika

¼ teaspoon onion powder

¼ teaspoon garlic powder

1 Preheat oven to 350°F. Coat 2 baking sheets with non-stick cooking spray or line with parchment paper.

2 Toss sweet potatoes with oil in a large bowl to coat.

3 Add salt, paprika, onion powder, and garlic powder; mix gently with your hands.

4 Spread sweet potatoes in a single layer on prepared baking sheets. (If they are too crowded, the fries won't crisp up.)

5 Bake until fries are tender, turning occasionally, about 20 minutes.

6 Increase heat to 475°F; bake 5 to 8 minutes, until nicely browned.

Makes 4 servings.

 TIP:

The fries taste best when eaten while they are still hot and crispy.

Per serving	Cal	Fat	Sat. Fat	Chol	Sodium	Carbs	Fiber	Sugar	Protein
Something Better	224	5g	0g	0mg	1188mg	42g	6g	0g	2g

Coconut Rice

Coconut rice is traditionally eaten with Indian and Thai foods, and it will quickly become a staple in your household. Kids love the great creamy texture—and adults love the spices. Try it with our Indian Dahl, or with any favorite stir-fry or veggie sauté recipe.

3 ½ cups water

2 cups brown basmati rice

1 can (15 ounce) coconut milk

1 tablespoon oil

1 tablespoon garlic, minced or paste

1 tablespoon ginger, minced or paste

1 teaspoon salt

¼ teaspoon ground turmeric

⅛ teaspoon ground cardamom

⅛ teaspoon ground coriander

1 Combine all ingredients in a medium saucepan. Bring to a boil over high heat.

2 Reduce to a simmer and cook, covered, 50 to 60 minutes, until rice is tender.

Makes 12 servings.

Per ½ cup serving	Cal	Fat	Sat. Fat	Chol	Sodium	Carbs	Fiber	Sugar	Protein
Something Better	**163**	**6g**	**4g**	**0mg**	**164mg**	**25g**	**1g**	**0g**	**3g**

Flaky Brown Rice

Brown rice is much better for you than white rice. It's higher in both fiber and protein, so it fills you up longer and gives sustained energy until your next meal.

2 cups brown rice

4 cups water

¾ teaspoon salt

1 Place rice in a dry skillet. Heat over medium-high, stirring frequently, until rice begins to pop and crackle. Continue to heat 2 to 3 minutes, stirring often.

2 Add water and salt to skillet; bring to a boil over high heat.

3 Reduce to a simmer; cover and cook 60 minutes.

Makes 10 servings.

CHANGE IT UP:

Cilantro Lime Rice: Mix 3 cups rice with 2 tablespoons lime juice, ½ cup fresh cilantro, and 1 teaspoon salt.

TIP:

It is very important not to PEEK or stir the rice while it is cooking or it will be sticky.

Spanish Rice

Whether you're making our Dominican Beans recipe or serving up your own Mexican meal, you won't want to forget the rice! Spanish rice is filled with colorful vegetables, and it's got lots of flavor.

2 cups brown rice

2 teaspoons oil

¼ large onion, finely chopped

¼ medium green or red pepper, finely chopped

¼ cup green Spanish olives, finely chopped

1 small tomato, finely chopped

2 cloves garlic

1 ½ teaspoons **Chicken Style Seasoning** (page 152) or commercial chicken seasoning

1 ½ teaspoons salt

½ teaspoon dried oregano

3 cups water

1 can (8 ounces) tomato sauce

1 Place rice in a dry medium skillet. Heat over medium-high, stirring frequently, until rice begins to pop and crackle. Continue to heat 2 to 3 minutes, stirring often. Remove toasted rice from skillet; set aside.

2 Heat oil over medium in a large skillet that has a tight-fitting lid.

3 Add onion, pepper, and olives to skillet; cook until onions are translucent, stirring occasionally.

4 Add tomatoes, garlic, chicken seasoning, salt, and oregano to skillet; cook 1 minute, stirring.

5 Add water and tomato sauce; bring to a boil over high heat.

6 Add reserved brown rice; stir and cover. Reduce heat to low and simmer 60 minutes. Don't PEEK!

Makes 12 servings.

TIP:

Toasting the rice first makes it flaky so it won't stick together like brown rice tends to do.

NOW & LATER:

While a perfect complement to Dominican Beans, the leftovers are great in the Bean & Rice Chimichanga (page 70) or as a side with other Mexican dishes. It also freezes well, so make extra.

Per ½ cup serving	Cal	Fat	Sat. Fat	Chol	Sodium	Carbs	Fiber	Sugar	Protein
Traditional Recipe	130	4g	1g	0mg	625mg	22g	1g	3g	3g
Something Better	**58**	**1g**	**0g**	**0mg**	**450mg**	**10g**	**1g**	**2g**	**2g**

Spring Rolls

Try these amazingly good spring rolls that are baked and not fried, so you can eat more!

2 tablespoons oil

1 medium onion, finely diced

½ cup vegetarian sausage or beef-style crumbles (optional)

8 cups cabbage, shredded

3 cups carrots, grated

¼ cup **Braggs Liquid Aminos** or low sodium soy sauce

1 tablespoon **Chicken Style Seasoning** (page 152) or commercial chicken seasoning

1 package (25 count) spring roll wrappers

1 Preheat oven to 350°F. Coat a large baking sheet with non-stick cooking spray.

2 Heat oil in a large skillet over medium heat; add onion and sausage. Cook until onion is softened, stirring occasionally, about 4 minutes.

3 Add cabbage, carrots, soy sauce, and chicken seasoning to skillet; cook until vegetables are crisp-tender. Remove from heat and allow to cool.

4 Follow directions on spring roll package to fill and roll the spring rolls. Place filled spring rolls on prepared baking sheet.

5 Gently coat tops of spring rolls with cooking spray.

6 Bake 15 to 20 minutes, until golden brown and crispy.

Makes 25 spring rolls.

 TIP:

Some of the spring roll wrappers have cholesterol so watch your labels!

 TIP:

The filling can be made ahead and stored in the refrigerator until ready to use.

Per 1 roll serving	Cal	Fat	Sat. Fat	Chol	Sodium	Carbs	Fiber	Sugar	Protein
Traditional Recipe	200	12g	4g	20mg	390mg	16g	2g	2g	8g
Something Better	**116**	**1g**	**0g**	**0mg**	**291mg**	**23g**	**2g**	**2g**	**4g**

Guilt-Free Guacamole

Adding beans to the avocados does great things to your guacamole. You get lots of added fiber, a lot less fat per serving, and your guacamole will stay green longer!

2 medium avocados, peeled and chopped

1 can (15 ounces) canned white beans, rinsed and drained

3 tablespoons lime or lemon juice

1 clove garlic, minced

½ teaspoon salt

¼ teaspoon ground cumin

½ cup red or green onion, minced

¼ cup tomatoes, finely diced

2 tablespoons cilantro, chopped (optional)

½ small jalapeño, finely chopped (optional)

1 Puree avocados and beans in a food processor.

2 Add lime or lemon juice, garlic, salt, and cumin to food processor; pulse until just blended.

3 Stir in remaining ingredients and serve.

Makes 3 cups.

Per ¼ cup serving	Cal	Fat	Sat. Fat	Chol	Sodium	Carbs	Fiber	Sugar	Protein
Traditional Recipe	120	10g	2g	0mg	180g	6g	4g	0g	2g
Something Better	**100**	**5g**	**0g**	**0mg**	**84mg**	**12g**	**4g**	**0g**	**4g**

Tostones

oil, for frying

3 plantains, peeled and sliced into 1-inch pieces

salt, to taste

1 Heat a large skillet over medium-high; add enough oil to generously cover bottom of the skillet.

2 Add plantains to skillet in a single layer; and cook until lightly golden in color on both sides, about 3 minutes. Drain on paper towels. Repeat with remaining slices.

3 While plantains are still warm, mash them with a glass or other flat surface to ¼-inch thick.

4 Return flattened slices to skillet; fry again until golden brown.

5 Drain on paper towels, season with salt, and serve.

Makes 10 servings.

Per 4 piece serving	Cal	Fat	Sat. Fat	Chol	Sodium	Carbs	Fiber	Sugar	Protein
Something Better	**189**	**9g**	**1g**	**0mg**	**4mg**	**29g**	**2g**	**13g**	**1g**

American Cheeze Sauce

Whether you're looking for a creamy sauce for steamed vegetables or a great dip, we've got just the recipe for you! Pour the warm Cheeze right over your veggies, or add a can of tomatoes with green chilies and serve with tortilla chips. You can use this sauce on anything you would use a traditional cheese sauce.

3 ½ cups water, divided

2 cups **raw cashews**

½ cup roasted red pepper or pimento

⅓ cup **nutritional yeast flakes**

¼ cup lemon juice

1 tablespoon salt

1 ½ tablespoons cornstarch

2 teaspoons onion powder

2 teaspoons paprika

¼ teaspoon garlic powder

1 Place 1 ½ cups water and remaining ingredients in a blender; blend until very smooth. Pour into a medium saucepan.

2 Add remaining 2 cups water to blender; blend briefly to clean out. Add to saucepan and stir.

3 Bring to a boil over medium heat, stirring constantly, until thick.

Makes 6 cups.

NOW & LATER:

Make a double batch and freeze half before thickening over the stove. Or use it in Mac & Cheese (page 92), Melty Muffins (page 38), or Cheezie Potatoes (page 119).

Per ¼ cup serving	Cal	Fat	Sat. Fat	Chol	Sodium	Carbs	Fiber	Sugar	Protein
Cheez Whiz	182	14g	9g	50mg	1082mg	6g	0g	4g	8g
American Cheeze	56	4g	0g	0mg	238mg	4g	0g	0g	3g

Melty Cheeze

Another great Cheeze sauce—be sure to try them both!

3 cups water, divided

½ cup roasted red pepper or pimento

2 tablespoons cornstarch

½ cup **raw cashews**

½ tablespoon salt

¼ cup **nutritional yeast flakes**

¼ cup quick-cooking oats

2 tablespoons lemon juice

1 ½ teaspoons onion powder

1 Place 2 cups water and remaining ingredients in a blender; blend until very smooth. Pour into a medium saucepan.

2 Add remaining 1 cup of water to blender; blend briefly to clean out. Add to saucepan.

3 Cook over medium heat until thick, stirring constantly.

Makes 4 cups.

TIP:

Blend 4 or 5 minutes to make sure your cashews are well blended. The sauce should become completely smooth and creamy.

Per ¼ cup serving	Cal	Fat	Sat. Fat	Chol	Sodium	Carbs	Fiber	Sugar	Protein
Cheez Whiz	182	14g	9g	50mg	1082mg	6g	0g	4g	8g
Melty Cheeze	34	2g	0g	0mg	180mg	4g	1g	0g	3g

Mushroom Gravy

1 tablespoon oil

1 package (12 ounces) fresh mushrooms, trimmed and cut into ½-inch pieces, or 13-ounce can mushrooms, drained

2 cloves garlic, minced

1 tablespoon **beef style seasoning**

1 teaspoon salt

¼ cup unbleached white flour

1 cup hot water

1 cup Silk **soy creamer**, plain, or unsweetened **nondairy milk**

1 Heat oil in a medium skillet over medium; add mushrooms and cook, stirring occasionally, until mushrooms begin to give up some of their liquid, about 5 minutes. If using canned mushrooms, stir until heated through.

2 Add garlic, beef style seasoning, and salt; stir to coat.

3 Sprinkle flour over mushrooms; cook 2 to 3 minutes, stirring occasionally.

4 Add water and creamer or milk to skillet; cook until gravy thickens, 6 to 8 minutes.

Makes 2 cups.

TIP:

Keeping the lumps out of your gravy can be a little tricky. Make sure when you sprinkle in the flour and brown it you get out all the lumps before adding the water.

Per ¼ cup serving	Cal	Fat	Sat. Fat	Chol	Sodium	Carbs	Fiber	Sugar	Protein
Something Better	64	4g	0g	0mg	443mg	5g	0g	0g	0g

Brown Gravy

Forget the gravy packets—they're loaded with excess salt and additives! Try a quick and easy homemade gravy instead—it's perfect over mashed potatoes!

⅓ cup unbleached white flour

2 cups water

½ small onion, chopped

2 tablespoons oil

2 tablespoons **Braggs Liquid Aminos** or low sodium soy sauce

½ tablespoon **beef style seasoning**

⅛ teaspoon salt, or to taste

1 Place flour in a dry small skillet; cook over medium heat until lightly browned, stirring constantly.

2 Transfer flour and remaining ingredients to a blender; blend until smooth.

3 Pour mixture into a medium saucepan; heat over medium until thick, stirring constantly to prevent lumps and burning.

Makes 2 ½ cups.

Per ¼ cup serving	Cal	Fat	Sat. Fat	Chol	Sodium	Carbs	Fiber	Sugar	Protein
Something Better	45	3g	0g	0mg	207mg	4g	0g	0g	0g

Fake Feta

Many people enjoy tangy feta cheese on salad, but our low-fat, cholesterol-free version is even better. If you are up for something new, try it on one of our unique Pizzas (page 101).

1 package (14 ounces) water-packed **tofu**, firm or extra-firm crumbled

½ cup lemon juice

¼ cup water

2 tablespoons olive oil

1 tablespoon dried basil

2 teaspoons salt

1 teaspoon onion powder

½ teaspoon garlic powder

1 Drain water off tofu. You want the tofu to be as dry as possible when making Fake Feta. (See TIP)

2 Whisk remaining ingredients together in a medium bowl.

3 Add tofu to bowl; stir and refrigerate at least an hour, but overnight is best.
Makes 2 cups.

TIP:

I like my feta a little firmer, so I usually crumble it, spread on a plate, and microwave it on high until it starts to make a popping sound. This removes a lot of the water, resulting in firmer tofu. The lemon juice helps it to firm up a little more.

Per ¼ cup serving	Cal	Fat	Sat. Fat	Chol	Sodium	Carbs	Fiber	Sugar	Protein
Feta Cheese (1 oz.)	75	6g	4g	25mg	316mg	1g	0g	1g	4g
Something Better	**72**	**4g**	**0g**	**0mg**	**476mg**	**3g**	**1g**	**0g**	**7g**

Basil Pesto

Rich and delicious Basil Pesto is one of those items where a little goes a long way because it is packed with so many flavors.

¼ cup walnuts

2 cups fresh basil

3 cloves garlic

1 tablespoon lemon juice

¼ cup olive oil

¼ cup **nondairy parmesan cheese** or **nutritional yeast flakes**

¼ teaspoon salt

1 Pulse walnuts in a food processor until fairly fine.

2 Add basil, garlic, and lemon juice. Pulse a few times, until coarsely chopped.

3 With machine running, slowly drizzle oil into walnut mixture.

4 Add cheese and salt; pulse until combined.
Makes ¾ cup.

TIP:

Sometimes, it's cheaper to buy a basil plant at the store than those little plastic containers. Plus, it lasts a lot longer!

Per 2 tablespoon serving	Cal	Fat	Sat. Fat	Chol	Sodium	Carbs	Fiber	Sugar	Protein
Traditional Recipe	160	15g	4g	12mg	210mg	2g	0g	0g	5g
Something Better	**142**	**12g**	**2g**	**0mg**	**80mg**	**4g**	**0g**	**0g**	**4g**

Ketchup

Did you know that regular ketchup has more sugar per cup than ice cream? It's true, and it is usually high fructose corn syrup—so we came up with this recipe that satisfies the craving but is much better for you.

1 can (6 ounces) tomato paste

⅓ cup lemon juice

⅓ cup water

2 tablespoons **cane juice crystals** or sugar

½ **to 1** teaspoon salt, to taste

½ teaspoon onion powder

⅛ teaspoon garlic powder

Combine all ingredients in a small bowl; whisk together until completely combined.

Makes 2 ½ cups.

Per 2 ½ cup serving	Cal	Fat	Sat. Fat	Chol	Sodium	Carbs	Fiber	Sugar	Protein
Ketchup	30	0g	0g	0mg	334mg	8g	0g	7g	1g
Something Better	**17**	**0g**	**0g**	**0mg**	**84mg**	**4g**	**0g**	**3g**	**0g**

Aioli

This is a nice creamy condiment that we often use in place of mayonnaise or sour cream. It works great in recipes; try it in the Tofu Ricotta (page 68), Breaded Eggplant (page 66) or one of our great salads.

1 cup Silk Soy Milk, unsweetened

1 ½ teaspoons salt

1 teaspoon onion powder

¼ teaspoon garlic powder

1 cup oil

3 tablespoons lemon juice

1 Place milk, salt, onion powder, and garlic powder in a blender. Blend on high; slowly drizzle in oil with machine running.

2 Pour mixture into a bowl; gently fold in lemon juice. Refrigerate.

Makes 2 cups.

 TIP:
This will thicken as it chills.

TIP:
Drizzling the oil slowly is the secret to great Aioli. It should take about 1 minute to add the oil.

Per 2 tablespoon serving	Cal	Fat	Sat. Fat	Chol	Sodium	Carbs	Fiber	Sugar	Protein
Mayonnaise	114	8g	1g	8mg	210mg	7g	0g	2g	0g
Something Better	**63**	**7g**	**0g**	**0mg**	**91mg**	**0g**	**0g**	**0g**	**0g**

WHERE ARE YOU
going?

You have decided to take a trip to visit a friend you haven't seen in years. The car is packed with suitcases and the kids are settled in with books and toys to keep them occupied. The GPS doesn't seem to be working, but that's okay. You don't have an address anyway. You are pretty sure you need to go south. Off you go—which way do you turn? Which road will get you to where you need to go?

It sounds absolutely crazy, doesn't it? The fact of the matter is that this is how many of us live our lives. We wake up, cook breakfast, do some laundry, go to work, come home, make supper, go to bed, and wake up just to do it all over again. There is no real purpose. We just try to make it through another day. That is not the case for those living in the Blue Zones, however. For these people, life is not just a daily routine—life is a journey driven by purpose.

Now I am sure you did not buy a cookbook to learn answer to the age old question, "What is the meaning of life?" The answer to that question, however, does play a key role in the health and longevity of people in America's Blue Zone.

The Adventists find purpose through the many opportunities they have to volunteer at church and at the thousands of community service centers, hospitals and schools that are operated by their church. More importantly, the Adventists believe that God has given them a purpose to share His message of hope, healing and wholeness with the world before His soon return. They have a passion to share God's great gift of life, salvation, and eternity with others. God is in the business of giving life—a healthful life here on this earth and a heavenly life to come.

Science backs all this up. Dr. Herold Koeing from Duke University states that, "People who feel their life is part of a larger plan and are guided by their spiritual values have stronger immune systems, lower blood pressure, a lower risk of heart attack and cancer, and heal faster and live longer." Although scientists have not figured it all out just yet, plenty of studies have shown that faith in God and regular church attendance can reduce chronic stress, alleviate depression, and prevent people from engaging in risky behaviors. In fact, research indicates that people who attend church live an average of 7 to 14 years longer than those who do not. Purpose is certainly an important part of the "Adventist Advantage."

What is your "road map?" Many have discovered that God gives personal direction for those who seek it. The Bible is the written word of God that can give direction in an uncertain world. Sit down with your family and explore the treasures found there. Consider where you are going in life and the best way to get there. By knowing where you are headed, you can make better choices and your family can have "something better," forever!

desserts

Save room for dessert!

We like to show love to our families by making them sweet treats. Unfortunately, too much sugar leads to obesity, diabetes, and other life-threatening illnesses, which are truly no way to show someone you love them! Instead, make a better sweet treat that's lower in sugar and made with whole grains. It is a good idea to serve desserts with the high fiber meal because it helps to stabilize blood sugar, and it gives your body a little extra nutrient boost. Now that's something to share with the family!

"He said to me, "Son of man, feed your stomach and fill your body with this scroll which I am giving you." Then I ate it, and it was sweet as honey in my mouth."

Ezekiel 3:3 ASB

Coconut Joy Bars

Very rich and delicious—these bars will remind you of a famous candy bar. You can always leave out the nuts if you want, because sometimes you feel like a nut and sometimes you don't!

FILLING

⅔ cup extra-firm silken **tofu**

⅔ cup **nondairy milk** or coconut milk

½ cup **carob chips**, barley malt sweetened

⅓ cup **cane juice crystals** or sugar

2 tablespoons cornstarch

TOPPING

1 cup shredded coconut, unsweetened

½ cup almonds or other nut, lightly toasted (optional)

1 Preheat oven to 350°F. Coat an 8-by-8-inch baking pan with non-stick cooking spray.

2 Press prepared crust evenly into bottom of prepared pan.

3 Place filling ingredients in a food processor; blend until smooth. Pour over unbaked crust.

4 Sprinkle coconut and nuts over filling; press gently into filling.

5 Bake 25 to 30 minutes, until lightly browned.

6 Allow to cool completely; cut into small bars and serve.

Makes 32 bars.

 TIP:

Remember to press the coconut and almonds into the filling or they will fall off.

Per 1 bar serving	Cal	Fat	Sat. Fat	Chol	Sodium	Carbs	Fiber	Sugar	Protein
Candy Bar	220	13g	8g	0mg	50mg	26g	2g	20g	2g
Something Better	**103**	**5g**	**2g**	**0mg**	**50mg**	**14g**	**0g**	**8g**	**2g**

Fruit and Coconut Bars

What's sweet enough for dessert and almost healthy enough for breakfast? Our Fruit and Coconut Bars! They're made with toasted coconut, fruits, and whole grains—you gotta love that!

BOTTOM

1 ¼ cups unsweetened coconut

¾ cup **whole wheat pastry flour**

⅛ teaspoon salt

¼ cup **nondairy milk**

¼ cup maple syrup

2 tablespoons oil

¼ teaspoon vanilla extract

FILLING

1 cup Fruit Sauce (page 7) or spreadable all-fruit jam

TOPPING

½ cup unsweetened coconut

¼ cup **whole wheat pastry flour**

1 ½ tablespoons oil

⅛ teaspoon salt

BOTTOM LAYER

1 Preheat oven to 350°F. Coat an 8-by-8-inch baking pan with non-stick cooking spray.

2 Combine coconut, flour, and salt in a medium bowl.

3 Whisk together milk, maple syrup, oil, and vanilla in a separate medium bowl.

4 Mix milk mixture into coconut mixture; press into prepared pan.

FRUIT LAYER

1 Heat jam in microwave for 30 seconds; pour over the prepared bottom layer. Alternatively, use leftover Fruit Sauce (no reheating required).

TOPPING

1 Combine topping ingredients in a medium bowl; using hands, mix together until resembles coarse crumbs.

2 Sprinkle topping over fruit layer; press gently.

3 Bake 28 to 30 minutes, until topping is light golden brown.

4 Allow to cool completely; cut into small bars and serve.

Makes 16 squares.

Per 1 square serving	Cal	Fat	Sat. Fat	Chol	Sodium	Carbs	Fiber	Sugar	Protein
Something Better	103	5g	2g	0mg	35mg	14g	2g	6g	2g

Carob Chunk Cookies

Our unbelievably good carob chunk cookies are made with whole grain flour. They don't even look like healthy cookies, much less taste like them!

1 ¾ cups **whole wheat pastry flour**

¼ cup **cane juice crystals** or sugar

2 teaspoons **aluminum-free baking powder**

½ teaspoon salt

WET INGREDIENTS

½ cup maple syrup

⅓ cup oil

1 teaspoon vanilla extract

EXTRAS

⅔ cup Awesome Fudge (page 147), cut into small chunks

½ cup chopped nuts (optional)

1 Preheat oven to 350°F. Coat a large baking sheet with non-stick cooking spray or line with parchment paper.

2 Mix dry ingredients together in a medium bowl.

3 Whisk wet ingredients together in a separate medium bowl.

4 Add wet mixture to dry mixture; mix until just combined.

5 Gently fold in Awesome Fudge chunks and nuts.

6 Scoop dough with a tablespoon to form balls; drop balls onto prepared baking sheet, about 2 inches apart each.

7 Bake 11 to 12 minutes, until cookies are just browned on the bottom. Cookies will be soft, but they will firm as they cool. Cool 5 minutes on baking sheet; transfer to a wire rack to cool completely.

Makes 24 cookies.

CHANGE IT UP:

Use the peppermint version of Awesome Fudge (page 147) for a wonderful peppermint fudge cookie!

Per 1 cookie serving	Cal	Fat	Sat. Fat	Chol	Sodium	Carbs	Fiber	Sugar	Protein
Chocolate Chip Cookie	196	10g	3g	0mg	119mg	26g	1g	14g	2g
Something Better	**125**	**7g**	**1g**	**0mg**	**49mg**	**16g**	**2g**	**7g**	**2g**

Pecan Doodle Cookies

Be sure to try this wonderful, subtly sweet cookie with the irresistible taste of toasted pecans!

SUGAR COATING

¼ cup **cane juice crystals** or sugar

1 teaspoon **carob powder** (optional)

¼ teaspoon ground cardamom (optional)

WET INGREDIENTS

¼ cup hot water

2 teaspoons ground **flax seeds**

½ cup **cane juice crystals** or sugar

¼ cup **non-hydrogenated margarine**

1 tablespoon vanilla extract

DRY INGREDIENTS

2 cups **whole wheat pastry flour**

1 tablespoon **aluminum-free baking powder**

½ teaspoon salt

½ teaspoon **Cinnamon Substitute** (page 152) or ¼ teaspoon ground coriander and ⅛ teaspoon ground cardamom

½ cup toasted pecans

1 Preheat oven to 350°F. Coat a large baking sheet with non-stick cooking spray or line with parchment paper.

2 Prepare sugar coating: combine all ingredients in a small bowl; set aside.

3 Whisk together hot water and flax seeds in a small bowl; set aside.

4 Combine cane juice crystals and margarine in a medium bowl; cream until thick and fluffy.

5 Add flax mixture and vanilla to margarine mixture; beat well.

6 Add dry ingredients to margarine mixture; mix until a dough has formed.

7 Scoop dough with a tablespoon to form balls; gently drop each ball into sugar coating mixture. Shake gently to coat; place on prepared baking sheet, about 2 inches apart each.

8 Bake 11 to 12 minutes, until cookies are lightly browned on the bottom. Cookies will still be soft, but they will firm as they cool. Cool 5 minutes on baking sheet; transfer to wire rack to cool completely.

Makes 40 cookies.

TIP:

Toast nuts in microwave on high 3 to 5 minutes, or in a preheated 350°F oven 10 minutes.

Per 1 cookie serving	Cal	Fat	Sat. Fat	Chol	Sodium	Carbs	Fiber	Sugar	Protein
Snicker doodle	140	5g	3g	10mg	95mg	22g	0g	9g	2g
Something Better	**103**	**5g**	**2g**	**0mg**	**35mg**	**14g**	**2g**	**6g**	**2g**

Peanut Buttery Cookies

You will not believe the peanut buttery goodness of these cookies. Natural peanut butter is the best because it has a pure peanutty taste with nothing added. If you are a fan of peanut butter and carob together, you MUST try the Peanut Butter Carob Bar version on the next page... absolutely fabulous!

DRY INGREDIENTS

2 cups quick-cooking oats

1 ⅓ cups **whole wheat pastry flour**

2 teaspoons **aluminum-free baking powder**

½ teaspoon salt

WET INGREDIENTS

⅔ cup **sucanat** or brown sugar

½ cup **natural peanut butter**

½ cup **nondairy milk**

⅓ cup oil

¼ cup **cane juice crystals** or sugar

4 teaspoons ground **flax seeds**

1 ½ teaspoons vanilla extract

EXTRAS

¼ to ½ cup **natural peanut butter**

1 Preheat oven to 350°F. Coat a large baking sheet with non-stick cooking spray or line with parchment paper.

2 Mix dry ingredients together in a medium bowl.

3 Whisk wet ingredients together in a separate medium bowl until smooth; add to dry mixture and mix until just combined.

4 Stirring by hand as you go, drop teaspoonfuls of the additional peanut butter into dough, mixing very lightly so that you have swirls of peanut butter throughout the dough.

5 Scoop dough with a tablespoon to form balls; drop balls onto prepared baking sheet, about 2 inches apart each, flattening slightly.

6 Bake 11 to 12 minutes, until cookies are just lightly browned around the edges. Cool 5 minutes on baking sheet; transfer to a wire rack to cool completely.

Makes 36 cookies.

CHANGE IT UP:

Peanut Buttery Carob Bar

1 recipe Peanut Buttery Cookies (page 139), dough unbaked

1 recipe Awesome Fudge (page 147), still hot and pourable

2 whole graham crackers, coarsely crushed

1 Preheat oven to 350°F. Coat an 8-by-8-inch baking pan with non-stick cooking spray or line with parchment paper.

2 Firmly press 1 ½ cups of prepared cookie dough into the bottom of prepared pan to make a ¼-inch crust.

3 Pour hot Awesome Fudge over crust; spread evenly.

4 Combine graham crackers and ¾ cup of prepared cookie dough in a medium bowl; mix well with hands until crumbly. Sprinkle over top of fudge, pressing down lightly.

5 Bake 20 to 25 minutes. Allow to cool completely; remove from pan and cut into small bars.

Makes 16 squares.

TIP:

You will still have enough cookie dough left over to make about a dozen Peanut Butter Cookies!

Per 1 cookie serving	Cal	Fat	Sat. Fat	Chol	Sodium	Carbs	Fiber	Sugar	Protein
Peanut Butter Cookie	119	6g	1g	0mg	104mg	15g	0g	8g	2g
Something Better	107	5g	0g	0mg	48mg	13g	2g	5g	3g

Lemon Pie

This easy lemon pie is a favorite go-to recipe when I need something quick.
My kids LOVE it. Thanks to Mary Bernt at Veggies for sharing it with us.

4 cups pineapple juice

⅔ cup cornstarch or arrowroot

½ cup lemon juice (fresh is best!)

½ cup honey

1 cup raspberries, fresh or frozen (optional)

1 prebaked Easy Pie Crust

1 Whisk pineapple juice and cornstarch together a medium saucepan to dissolve.

2 Add lemon juice and honey to pineapple mixture; bring to a boil over high heat, stirring constantly until well thickened. Remove from heat.

3 Gently place berries on prepared crust; carefully pour warm lemon mixture over berries. Refrigerate until well set.

Makes one 8-inch pie.

EASY PIE CRUST

11 sheets graham crackers or

1 ½ cups Granola (page 14)

3 tablespoons honey (eliminate if using granola)

2 tablespoons oil

1 Preheat oven to 350°F.

2 Grind graham crackers or Granola in a food processor until fine.

3 Combine graham crackers, honey, and oil together in a small bowl; mix well.

4 Press mixture into a 9-inch pie plate.

5 Bake 10 to 12 minutes, until edges just begin to brown.

Makes one 9-inch pie.

 TIP:

To serve a crowd, you can make this into bars by pressing the crust into a 9-by-13-inch pan instead of a pie plate.

Per 1/12 of pie serving	Cal	Fat	Sat. Fat	Chol	Sodium	Carbs	Fiber	Sugar	Protein
Lemon Meringue Pie	367	12g	2g	62mg	200mg	65g	2g	33g	2g
Something Better	**212**	**4g**	**0g**	**0mg**	**88mg**	**45g**	**1g**	**28g**	**1g**

Fantastic Vanilla Pudding

Who doesn't love pudding? You can do so much with it! You can use it in a Breakfast Parfait (page 13), or how about a Banana Cream Pie? You can use it in anything that you would use traditional vanilla pudding in. This pudding makes it fantastic! And it is so easy, too!

4 cups **nondairy milk**

⅔ cup cornstarch

¼ cup maple syrup

1 teaspoon salt

2 tablespoons vanilla extract

1 Combine all ingredients, except vanilla, in a medium saucepan. Stir well to eliminate lumps.

2 Heat over medium until mixture comes to a boil and thickens, stirring constantly.

3 Stir in vanilla. Cover and chill.

4 Before serving, blend mixture in a food processor for a smooth and creamy pudding.

Makes 8 servings.

 CHANGE IT UP:

Banana Cream Pie: Layer bananas and pudding in a prebaked pie shell. Top with non-dairy whipped topping for a perfect dessert.

 TIP:

Maple syrup can be very expensive, so if you don't want to use maple syrup, use a different sweetener and add ½ teaspoon maple flavoring.

 CHANGE IT UP:

Southern Style Banana Pudding: Make your favorite banana pudding recipe, using Fantastic Vanilla Pudding and whole grain vanilla wafers from your health food store.

Per ½ cup serving	Cal	Fat	Sat. Fat	Chol	Sodium	Carbs	Fiber	Sugar	Protein
Traditional Recipe	147	4g	2g	8mg	153mg	25g	0g	23g	3g
Something Better	**142**	**2g**	**0g**	**0mg**	**299mg**	**25g**	**0g**	**11g**	**4g**

Carob Cupcakes

A wonderfully moist cake that is sometimes called Wacky Cake because it doesn't have any eggs.

DRY INGREDIENTS

1 cup **cane juice crystals** or sugar

1 cup unbleached all-purpose flour

½ cup white **whole wheat pastry flour**

¼ cup Chatfield's Roasted **carob powder** (we highly recommend this brand because its flavor is the best)

1 teaspoon baking soda

½ teaspoon salt

WET INGREDIENTS

⅓ cup oil

1 cup water

1 tablespoon lemon juice

1 teaspoon vanilla extract

1 Preheat oven to 350°F. Coat muffin tins with non-stick cooking spray or line with cupcake liners.

2 Combine dry ingredients in a large bowl; stir and make a well in the center of the mixture.

3 Whisk together all wet ingredients in a medium bowl; pour carefully into the prepared well in dry flour mixture.

4 Whisk all ingredients together until smooth.

5 Fill each muffin cup approximately ⅔ full.

6 Bake 25 minutes, until a toothpick inserted in the middle comes out clean.

Makes 12 cupcakes.

TIP:

You can use cocoa powder in this recipe if you like, but you will need to increase the sugar because **carob** is sweeter than cocoa.

TIP:

Double this recipe to make a 9-by-13-inch cake.

TIP:

To make a carob cake, pour cupcake batter into a greased 8-inch round cake pan. Bake 25 to 30 minutes, until a toothpick inserted in the middle comes out clean.

Per 1 cupcake serving	Cal	Fat	Sat. Fat	Chol	Sodium	Carbs	Fiber	Sugar	Protein
Chocolate Cupcake	164	5g	1g	14mg	176mg	29g	1g	22g	2g
Something Better	**125**	**7g**	**1g**	**0mg**	**50mg**	**16g**	**2g**	**7g**	**2g**

Amazing Fudge

This fudge is AMAZING because it can be transformed into an infinite number of delicious treats—you are only limited by your imagination. Check out the next page with some "CHANGE IT UPs" to get you started.

½ cup **natural peanut butter**

1 ½ cups **carob chips**

1 Spread peanut butter all over the inside of a medium glass bowl so that you have a "peanut butter bowl."

2 Add carob chips to bowl, making sure that no carob chips touch the sides of the bowl.

3 Microwave on high 1 to 1 ½ minutes.

4 Remove from microwave and stir vigorously with a spoon until smooth. Chips will look glossy, not melted, until they are thoroughly stirred—be patient! If they don't completely melt, you may put them back in the microwave, but only for 10 seconds at a time. Carob chips burn very easily.

5 Pour into a plastic wrap-lined pan and chill.

6 Remove from pan and cut into squares.

Makes16 servings.

TIP:

If you don't want to use a microwave, you can use a double boiler to melt your **carob chips**, but be careful since **carob** burns easily.

CHANGE IT UP:

- Add 1 cup chopped walnuts or pecans.
- Add ½ cup toasted coconut and ½ cup toasted almonds.
- Add 1 cup raisins and ½ cup chopped nuts.
- Add 1 teaspoon peppermint flavoring.
- Add 1 teaspoon orange or raspberry flavoring.
- Add 1 cup soy milk powder and ½ teaspoon peppermint flavoring.

CAROB CURLS: Keep a bar of fudge in your freezer to make beautiful carob curls to garnish desserts. Using a vegetable peeler, gently "peel" the edge of the bar to make the curls. Once the curls are made, put them into the freezer to harden up again until you need them. Pictures on page 144.

NO BAKE COOKIES: Add 1 ½ cups lightly toasted quick oats and ½ cup of coconut. Drop onto wax paper by the tablespoon, then refrigerate until firm.

THIN MINT COOKIES: Dip graham crackers into the hot Amazing Fudge with 1 teaspoon peppermint flavoring added. Place on wax paper and cool. If you want to make them festive, put some crushed candy canes on each one before they harden.

RICE CRISPY TREATS: Mix in 6 cups of crisp rice cereal and press into a 9-by-13-inch pan lined with plastic wrap.

Per 2 piece serving	Cal	Fat	Sat.			Sodium	Carbs	Fiber	Sugar	Protein
Something Better	100	7g	3g			37mg	9g	1g	4g	3g

How to Cook Dry Beans

SORT

Place beans in a colander and wash under running water, looking through them for small rocks or pebbles and discolored or broken beans.

SOAK

Soaking beans shortens the cooking time and makes them more digestible. There are two basic methods for soaking. There are two basic methods of soaking.

The Long Soak: Simply cover the beans in water and soak them overnight, about 8 to 10 hours. You don't want to soak the beans more than 10 hours, for they can absorb too much liquid and lose their texture and flavor. If, however, you have soaked your beans and want to wait to cook them, drain the beans and store in the fridge until you're ready.

The Quick Soak: Put the beans in a large pot, add water and bring to a boil. Let the water boil about 2 minutes, then remove from heat, cover, and let soak for about 1 hour.

COOK

No matter which method you used for soaking, you want to use fresh water to cook the beans. Some recipes will have you add seasonings at this point, but adding salt now will increase your cook time.

Stove Top Method: Use a large pot, taking into account that the beans will expand quite a bit when they cook (1 cup of dried beans is about 3 cups cooked), so make sure you add enough water, about an inch and a half above the beans. Cook them at a gentle simmer and not a rolling boil. How long your beans will need to cook depends on how long they soaked, as well as their size. They can take anywhere from 1 ½ to 3 hours to become soft. Try them out as they're cooking until they achieve a perfect softness.

Crock Pot Method: Pour the soaked beans into your slow cooker. Be sure that you leave a few inches of clearance at the top of your slow cooker. Add enough fresh water so the beans are covered by an inch or two. Cover and set the slow cooker for 6 to 8 hours or overnight.

 TIP:

Never add tomatoes or any acidic ingredient to your beans until after they are soft, or they will never get soft.

miscellaneous

How to Prepare Soy Curls

4 cups hot water

3 cups **Soy Curls**

1 tablespoon oil

1 small onion, diced

¼ cup **Chicken Style Seasoning**

Salt, to taste

1 Soak Soy Curls in hot water 10 minutes. Drain.

2 Sauté Soy Curls, onion, and Chicken Style Seasoning in a small amount of oil until dark brown.

How to Blend Cashews

Cashews are soft nuts that make a rich cream when blended with water. If blended right, your cashew cream can be silky smooth. Here's what you do:

1 Place cashews in blender with just enough water to blend.

2 Blend for several minutes, until completely smooth.

3 Rub a small amount between your fingers. You should feel no grittiness at all.

How to Drain Tofu

Draining tofu is simply removing excess water from the tofu. Draining makes the tofu firmer and cook faster. If you don't drain the tofu it will take longer to brown. Pour water off of the tofu and try one of these methods to drain the tofu.

◆ Place tofu in a colander. Place a plate over the tofu and place something heavy on the plate so that the tofu is being pressed. Allow tofu to drain 30 minutes.

◆ Wrap tofu tightly in a large lint-free towel; place in the refrigerator for several hours or overnight.

◆ Microwaving drained tofu for a few minutes will draw out some of the water; finish by blotting with a paper towel.

How to Roll Pie Crust

1 With a damp cloth, moisten an area about 12-by-14-inches. Place plastic wrap over wet area. (The dampness under the plastic will help hold it in place and keep it from sliding around while you roll out the dough.)

2 Put dough in the center of the plastic wrap; place another piece of plastic wrap over the dough.

3 Roll out a 10-by-14-inch rectangle or 12-inch circle.

4 Remove top plastic. Carefully lift the bottom plastic and gently place over the pot pie. Trim to fit the pan or fold in edges and flute like a traditional pie.

5 Bake one hour, or until fluted edge is firm.

Light and Fluffy Pancake Mix

9 cups **whole wheat pastry flour**

3 cups unbleached white flour

3 cups cornmeal

⅔ cup **nondairy milk** powder

⅓ cup **cane juice crystals** or sugar

⅓ cup **aluminum-free baking powder**

1 tablespoon salt

1 Mix all ingredients in a large airtight container.

2 To make pancakes, add 2 ½ cups of mix to 2 cups water and ¼ cup oil. Mix well.

3 Using a ⅓ cup measure, pour onto a hot griddle and cook until golden.

4 Flip over and cook the other side until golden.

Makes 12 recipes.

Breading Mix

2 ¾ cups **whole wheat flour**

2 cups cornmeal

2 cups **nutritional yeast flakes**

⅔ cup **non-dairy parmesan cheese** (optional)

¼ cup parsley flakes

2 tablespoons salt

2 tablespoons onion powder

1 ¼ tablespoons paprika

1 ½ tablespoons dried basil

¾ tablespoons garlic powder

1 Mix all ingredients in an airtight container.

Makes 7 cups.

Scrambled Tofu Seasoning Mix

2 cups **nutritional yeast flakes**

1 ½ cups **Chicken Style Seasoning** (page 152) or commercial brand

¼ cup garlic powder

2 ¾ tablespoons onion powder

2 ¾ tablespoons salt

2 teaspoons ground turmeric

1 Mix all ingredients in an airtight container.

2 Add ½ cup mix to 2 packages (14 ounces) of tofu and cook according to the directions for Scrambled Tofu (page 10).

Makes 8 recipes of Scrambled Tofu.

Taco Seasoning Mix

2 cups flour (whole wheat, white, or oat)

½ cup chili powder

⅓ cup ground cumin

¼ cup salt

2 tablespoons onion powder

1 ½ tablespoons paprika

2 teaspoons garlic powder

1 teaspoon cayenne pepper

1 Mix all ingredients together.

2 Store in an airtight container.

Makes 2 ⅔ cups.

Country Style Seasoning

This seasoning mix makes the Vegetable Pot Pie (page 50) great! It can be used as a **Chicken Style Seasoning** substitute, but it will give a little different flavor.

1 ½ cups **nutritional yeast flakes**

3 tablespoons salt

1 tablespoon onion powder

1 tablespoon paprika

1 tablespoon **sucanat** or **cane juice crystals**

2 teaspoons garlic powder

1 teaspoon dried parsley

½ teaspoon celery seed

½ teaspoon ground turmeric

1 Blend all ingredients in a blender until very fine.

2 Store in an airtight container.

Makes 2 cups

Cinnamon Substitute

Wondering why you would want a substitute for cinnamon? Look it up in the glossary (page 165).

¼ cup ground coriander

2 tablespoons ground cardamom

1 Mix ingredients together.

2 Store in an airtight container.

3 Use as a substitute for cinnamon in any recipe.

Chicken Style Seasoning

4 cups **nutritional yeast flakes**

⅔ cup onion powder

⅔ cup salt

½ cup Italian seasoning (no salt added)

⅓ cup dried parsley

¼ cup **sucanat** or **cane juice crystals**

3 tablespoons garlic powder

1 ½ teaspoons celery seed

¾ teaspoon cayenne pepper

1 Blend all ingredients in a blender until very fine.

2 Store in an air tight container.

Makes 4 ½ cups

 TIP:

To make broth, add 1 tablespoon of **Chicken Style Seasoning** mix to 1 cup of water.

SOMETHING BETTER in your recipes

Don't give up your family's favorite recipes—just make them better with these easy substitutions (you don't even have to tell them!).

IF YOU USUALLY USE...	TRY SOMETHING BETTER...	WHERE TO FIND IT
Bread	Whole wheat or multigrain bread	Local grocery
Brown sugar	Sucanat	Large grocery: baking aisle
Butter	Non-hydrogenated margarine	Local grocery: dairy aisle
Cheese slices or shreds	Soy or rice cheeses or Melty Cheeze (page 127) and American Cheeze Sauce (page 127)	Local grocery: produce department
Chocolate	Carob chips; carob powder	Health food store
Chicken or beef broth	Vegetable broth or 1 cup water mixed with 1 tablespoon Chicken Style Seasoning	Local grocery: soup aisle
Coffee	Kaffree Roma, Bueno	Health food store
Eggs (in baking)	Flax seed gel: 1 egg = 1 tablespoon ground flax seeds mixed with 3 tablespoons hot water	Local grocery or health food store
	Ener-G egg replacer: see package directions	
	Cornstarch: 1 egg = 1 tablespoon	
	Tofu: 1 egg = ¼ cup blended	
Mayonnaise	Aioli (page 130) Vegenaise (our favorite) or Nayonaise	Health food store, some local grocery: produce aisle
Meat (chicken, lunchmeats, beef, sausage, hotdogs)	Light Life, Morning Star Farms Meal Starters, Boca, Yves, Tofurky, Gardien, Gluten Steaks (page 48), Pre-pared Soy Curls (page150)	Local grocery: frozen and produce aisle; more options at the health food store
Milk	Nondairy soy milk, almond milk, rice milk, etc.	Local grocery: dairy aisle
Parmesan cheese	Soy or nut cheese (Soymage "Vegan" is our favorite)	Health food store: refrigerated aisle
Pasta	Whole wheat or multigrain pasta	Local grocery
Peanut butter	Natural peanut butter, almond butter, cashew butter, or sunflower seed butter	Local grocery
Sour cream	Tofutti Sour Cream or other brand or Aioli (page 130)	Health food store, some local grocery: dairy aisle
Soy sauce	Bragg's Liquid Aminos	Health food store
Sugar	Cane juice crystals, honey, agave nectar	Local grocery: baking aisle
White flour	Whole wheat pastry flour (for cookies, cakes, etc.)	Large grocery chain, health food store: baking aisle

Portion Your Plate

People in the Blue Zones don't have to count calories and carbs—they simply guard their portions. Here is an easy way to be sure that you get a good balanced diet: fill half of your plate with fruits or vegetables, one-fourth with whole grains or high carbohydrate vegetables like potatoes and corn, and the last quarter of your plate should be protein such as beans, tofu, nuts and meat substitutes.

The Adventist Lifestyle promotes regular meals, with breakfast being the heartiest meal of the day. Try to have at least 4 to 5 hours between meals to give the digestive system time to rest. Have supper at least 4 hours before bedtime for a more restful sleep. When you do this, you will wake up with a healthy appetite, ready for breakfast. Some people think that they should not eat breakfast because "I'm just not hungry." If you have an early, light supper, you will most likely be hungry and ready for a healthful breakfast to get your body and brain off to a great start.

Color Your Plate Like a Rainbow!

You now see the secret of America's Blue Zone and how the Adventists are living longer and more vibrant lives. You can do this too! The answer is simple—color your plate like a rainbow!

RED

can help lower your blood pressure, reduce the risk of prostate cancer, lower LDL cholesterol levels, and reduce tumor growth.

Cherries   Strawberries
Cranberries   Tomatoes
Grapes   Watermelons
Raspberries   Radishes
Red beans   Red bell
Grapefruits   peppers

ORANGE AND YELLOW

promote healthy joints and help build stronger bones.

Apricots   Oranges
Bell peppers   Peaches
Cantaloupes   Pumpkin
Carrots   Squash
Sweet potatoes   Apples
 Lemons

When serving your family plant-based meals, have fun and "mix it up" to create meals that are as colorful as they are delicious. Add a variety of colorful fruits, vegetables, nuts, and legumes to your meals. Each color provides an array of phytonutrients, providing the nutrition that each person in your family needs. Add blueberries or strawberries to your cereal; make a fresh salad with red leaf lettuce, red and yellow peppers, cucumbers, tomatoes, and black olives; and serve brilliant colored vegetables, such as sweet potatoes or broccoli spears. Just like painting a canvas, create color on your plate—and watch your family members' faces light up as you sit down to enjoy good food and good times together.

GREEN

fights free radicals, boosts immune system, normalizes digestion times, and supports retinal health.

Alfalfa sprouts	Green bell peppers
Artichokes	Green beans
Asparagus	Kale
Avocados	Lima beans
Broccoli	Pears
Brussels	Apples
sprouts	Grapes
Cabbage	Kiwi
Dark lettuces	Spinach

BLUE AND PURPLE

can fight inflammation and limit the activity of cancer cells.

Acai berries	Pomegranates
Beets	Grapes
Blackberries	Plums
Blueberries	Prunes
Cabbage	Red/purple
Eggplants	lettuces

WHITE

can balance hormone levels and reduce the risk of hormone-related cancers.

Bananas	Garlic
Bok choy	Navy beans
Cabbage	Onions
Cauliflower	Potatoes
Chickpeas	Turnips

What's For Dinner?

You're standing in front of the refrigerator with the door hanging open, just staring at the contents and trying to figure out what to feed the kids (who think they are starving). You could just order pizza again, but you made a promise to yourself that you would cook healthier meals. Unfortunately, promises are easier made than kept.

Does this scenario sound familiar? You're not alone. We all do it. Although the steps offered in this book are nothing new, we hope they will inspire you to keep your promises to offer your family healthy meals. Implementing them in your home will answer the age-old question: "What's for dinner?"

STEP 1 – MAKE TRADITIONS

Kids love traditions, and they like to know what to expect at the dinner table. Let that work to your advantage. It is always easier and faster to cook the same old things. Most of us eat about 12 different meals. That's it…12 meals. So just starting with one a week can quickly help you get acquainted with a new easy, delicious family favorite.

Use themes to make your menu planning easier. This book has seven themes, one for each day of the week. For example, Monday can be Soup and Sandwich day, Tuesday can be Almost Meat and Potatoes day, Wednesday can be set aside for Mexican Meals, etc.

STEP 2 – MAKE EVERYBODY'S FAVORITE

Get a calendar that you can write on, and determine which themes will be assigned to which days of the week. Now ask each family member to give you a list of their 3 favorite meals. Figure out where these meals fit into your daily themes and fill them in on the calendar. Everyone will be happy to see their favorite meals planned during the month.

If your family's favorite meals aren't in this cookbook, don't worry. You can check out our substitutions section and learn how to make your own recipes a little healthier.

Try new recipes gently. Choose one day a week to try a new plant-based meal from the recipes in this book and soon your whole calendar will be filled with healthy food that your family loves.

Another tip is to be sneaky…don't tell them that you prepared the recipe/dish differently. For example, if you are making your famous "Killer Chili," try using a bit of vegetarian burger and see if they notice. If not, you just got one step closer to a plant-based diet.

STEP 3 – GO SHOPPING

Go through your recipe calendar and make a grocery list. Remember to keep things on hand for emergency quick fixes. Just in case, we have a list of things you should have on page 164.

We have posted some weekly meal plans and grocery lists on our website for you to use if you like.

Creating healthy and delicious meals is fun and rewarding. With just a little planning, you can stop cooling the house with the fridge and you and your family can enjoy "something better" for dinner.

Breakfast Menus

Here is a sample of a four breakfast rotation that you can use as a guideline. You can check out our blog (http:// givethemsomethingbetter.blogspot.com) to see a few of our meal plans or download a blank meal planning worksheet. Remember to choose fresh fruit in season from a local farmer's market if you have one nearby and don't be afraid to try a fruit you haven't tried before. Fresh peaches, nectarines, plums, pears, pluots—whatever is on sale, try it!

	SUNDAY	MONDAY	TUESDAY	WEDNESDAY	THURSDAY	FRIDAY	SABBATH
WEEK 1	Light & Fluffy Pancakes Page 3	Hot Cereal Page 17	Cold cereal, whole grain toast, nut butter, orange	Toast & Gravy Page 11	Parfaits Page 13	Whole grain bagel and soy cream cheese, fruit salad sprinkled with sliced almonds.	Crockpot Oatmeal Page 17
WEEK 2	Citrus French Toast Page 5	Cold Cereal, soy yogurt, almonds, blueberries	Granola Page 13	Cold Cereal, whole grain English muffin all-fruit jam, grapes	Hot Cereal Page 17	Banana Muffins, cold cereal, fruit salad with soy yogurt dressing Page 21	Peach blueberry crisp Page 16
WEEK 3	Light and Fluffy Waffles Page 3	Cold cereal, whole grain English muffin, nut butter, apple	Breakfast Burrito Page 9	Toast & Gravy Page 11	Hot Cereal Page 17	Apple Pecan Muffins, whole grain toast , nut butter and all-fruit jam, fruit salad Page 19	Crockpot Oatmeal Page 17
WEEK 4	Scrambled Tofu, Oven Roasted Potatoes Page 9	Cold cereal, whole grain toast, all-fruit jam, pineapple	Hot Cereal Page 17	Cold Cereal, soy yogurt, walnuts, apple	Hot Cereal Option Page 17	Bagel and soy cream cheese, fruit salad sprinkled with sliced almonds	Apple Crisp Page 16

Main Meal Menus

This meal plan shows all of our main recipes in a 5-week rotation. There is a new recipe for each day of the week for 5 weeks. I believe this is way too much for the average mom to cook, but we wanted to include this so that you can see the scope of recipes and variety all in one place. This does not include the many CHANGE IT UPs throughout the book, which give even more variety.

	SUNDAY Soup & Sandwich	MONDAY Meat & Potatoes	TUESDAY Italian	WEDNESDAY Mexican	THURSDAY International	FRIDAY Junk Food	SABBATH Sharing Meals
WEEK 1	Split Pea Soup Chicken Salad Sandwich Page 46	Special T Loaf Cheezie Potatoes Page 52	Spaghetti & Meatballs Page 57	Tacos/Tostada Page 77	Szechwan Chicken Page 88	Pizza Page 99	Baked Potato Bar Page 114
WEEK 2	Minestrone & Meatball Subs Page 40	Chicken Stew Easy Biscuits Page 56	Pasta Primavera Page 60	Chilaquiles Page 72	Dominican Beans & Rice Page 84 & 124	Veggie Sub Potato Salad Page 94	Haystacks Page 111
WEEK 3	Corn Chowder & Melty Muffins Page 38	Gluten Steaks Mashed Potatoes Page 48	Lasagna Page 62	Bean & Rice Chimichanga Page 70	Pancit Spring rolls Page 90	BBQ Chicken Cole Slaw Page 96	Tater Tot Casserole Page 106
WEEK 4	White Chili & Veggie Wrap Page 42	Oatmeal Patties Green bean casserole Page 54	Eggplant Parmesan Page 66	Veggie Fajita Page 76	General Chows Tofu Page 82	Better Burgers Steak Fries Page 98	Pasta Bar Page 110
WEEK 5	Lentil Vegetable Egg Salad Page 44	Vegetable Pot Pie Page 50	Pasta with Spring Vegetables Page 64	Veggie Burrito Page 74	Dahl Page 186	Mac & Cheese Page 92	Mexican Lasagna Page 108

This is a typical menu plan that you could be found posted on your refrigerator. We have some built-in Quickie Days, and if your family likes leftovers you can schedule a leftover day once a week to clean out the fridge. I like to schedule Leftover Day on my errand day. This way, I have food ready when I get home and I am not tempted to go through the drive thru or pick up a pizza.

SUNDAY Soup & Sandwich	MONDAY Meat & Potatoes	TUESDAY Italian	WEDNESDAY Mexican	THURSDAY International	FRIDAY & SABBATH PREP Junk Food & Sharing Meals	
1 Split Pea Soup Chicken Salad	**2** Drive car pool Leftover day Make Granola	**3** Pasta Primavera	**4** Breakfast: Toast & Gravy Bean and Rice Chimichanga	**5** Breakfast- Granola Par- fait Pancit & Spring Rolls	**6** BBQ Chicken Sandwich Sweet Potato Fries	**7** Invite visi- tors over af- ter church Pasta Bar Dessert-Ba- nana Pudding
8 Breakfast: Citrus French Toast Quick Min- estrone Soup and Grilled Soy Cheese Sandwiches	**9** Gluten Steaks Mashed Pota- toes	**10** Piano Recital 6:30 Chicken Parmesan (Use QUICK TIP)	**11** Veggie Fajitas	**12** General Chow's Tofu	**13** Pesto Pizza	**14** Potluck at church Tater Tot Casserole Dessert-Fruit and Coconut Bars
15 Lentil Vegetable Soup Eggless Egg salad Sand- wiches	**16** Chicken Stew, Easy Biscuits, All-Amer- ican Salad Breakfast- Scrambled Tofu	**17** Breakfast: Breakfast Burrito & Gravy Spaghetti and Meatballs	**18** LEFTOVER DAY!	**19** Dad's B-day! Meet at Chi- nese Restau- rant at 5:30	**20** Veggie Subs Potato Salad	**21** Stuffed Shells Make extra-the Smiths are coming over for lunch. They are bring- ing dessert!
22 White Chili, Avocado Wrap	**23** Special T Loaf, Cheezie Potatoes, LIN- DA'S SUR- GERY Make a double batch to bring to Linda's family	**24** Lasagna	**25** Chilaquiles	**26** Dominican Beans Spanish Rice	**27** Macaroni & Cheeze	**28** Haystacks

Week 1

Once you have your monthly calendar in place, you can work on your weekly meal plan and plan ahead for the week.
We don't plan a breakfast every day, so if it isn't listed we just do cold cereal and fresh fruit.

Weekly Meal Plan for Week Beginning _9/3/2017_

	MEAL PLAN	PLANNING AHEAD
SUNDAY Soup & Sandwich	Breakfast: Pancakes & Fruit Sauce Split Pea Soup, Chicken Salad, whole wheat bread, lettuce, tomato and onion slices for sandwiches, All-American Salad	Make Prepared Soy Curls x2 (Extra for BBQ Chicken Sandwich-Friday) Planning for leftovers tomorrow. See what we have, if need be, make extra soup. Put oats in the crock pot for breakfast.
MONDAY Meat & Potatoes	Drive the car pool. Eat leftovers.	Make Garlic Spread x2 (for Garlic Bread on Tuesday and Week 2). Make Granola to have on hand.
TUESDAY Italian	Pasta Primavera, Spinach Salad, and Garlic Bread	Make Alfredo Sauce x2 (extra for Pasta Bar on Saturday)/Cut extra cauliflower, broccoli and carrots (for Pasta Bar on Saturday). Make Nut Gravy for breakfast.
WEDNESDAY Mexican	Bean and Rice Chimichanga, shredded lettuce, diced tomato, Aioli, Guilt-Free Guacamole, tortilla chips, and Salsa	Make Refried Beans x2 (freeze extra for Veggie Fajitas in Week 2)/ Spanish Rice x2 (freeze extra for Veggie Fajitas in Week 2)/Aioli x2 (extra for Coleslaw on Friday).
THURSDAY International	Breakfast: Granola Parfait Main Meal: Pancit, Spring Rolls	Fantastic Vanilla Pudding x2 (Extra for Banana Pudding on Sabbath dessert)/Shred extra cabbage (for Coleslaw on Friday).
FRIDAY Junk Food	BBQ Chicken Sandwich, Coleslaw, Sweet Potato Fries Prepare Pasta Bar for Sabbath Dessert: Banana Pudding	Use Prepared Soy Curls for BBQ Chicken Sandwich (from Sunday)/ Use shredded cabbage for Coleslaw (from Thursday)/Use Aioli for Coleslaw (from Wednesday). Make Basil Pesto x2 (freeze extra for Pesto Pizza in Week 2)/Use Alfredo Sauce (from Tuesday)/Use cut cauliflower, broccoli and carrots (from Tuesday)/Use Fantastic Vanilla Pudding for Banana Pudding (from Thursday).
SABBATH Sharing Meals	Cook Pasta and warm the sauces.	Rest.

Week 2

Weekly Meal Plan for Week Beginning _9/10/2017_

	MEAL PLAN	PLANNING AHEAD
SUNDAY Soup & Sandwich	Quick Meal: Tomato Soup and Grilled Soy Cheese Sandwiches	Peel and cube potatoes (for mashed potatoes on Monday). Store in a bowl of water in the refrigerator so they won't discolor.
MONDAY Meat & Potatoes	Gluten Steaks, mashed potatoes, Brown Gravy, steamed baby carrots, Spinach Salad	Make Gluten Steaks x 4 (extra for Veggie Fajitas on Wednesday and Tater Tot Casserole on Sabbath. Freeze for Chicken Stew and Chilaquiles in Week 3)/Make Brown Gravy x2 (extra for Tater Tot Casserole on Sabbath.
TUESDAY Italian	Piano Recital: 6:30 Make Chicken Parmesan with frozen Boca Chicken Patties and jarred spaghetti sauce, Italian Salad, Garlic Bread	Use Garlic Spread (from Week 1)/ Take Spanish Rice & refried beans out of the freezer so they can thaw (for Wednesday).
WEDNESDAY Mexican	Veggie Fajitas, shredded lettuce, diced tomato, Salsa, Aioli, Guilt-Free Guacamole, tortilla chips, Spanish Rice	Cut extra peppers and onions for Pesto Pizza-Friday/Use Gluten Steaks for Mexican Chicken (from Monday)/Use Refried Beans (frozen from Week 1)/Use Spanish Rice (frozen from Week 1).
THURSDAY International	Breakfast: Pancakes with Fruit Sauce Main Meal: General Chow's Tofu, Flaky Brown Rice, Cabbage Salad	Make Fruit Sauce x2 (extra for Fruit and Coconut Bars on Sabbath dessert)/Take Basil Pesto out of the freezer so it can thaw for Friday. Make Banana Muffins for breakfast.
FRIDAY Junk Food	Pesto Pizza, All-American Salad Make Tater Tot Casserole & Fruit and Coconut Bars (for Sabbath)	Use Basil Pesto (frozen from Week 1)/Use cut peppers and onions from Wednesday. Use Gluten Steaks (from Monday)/Use Brown Gravy (From Monday)/Use Fruit Sauce for Fruit and Coconut Bars(From Thursday).
SABBATH Sharing Meals	Place casserole in 250°F oven before church service. Remember to turn the oven up to 400°F right after church to crisp up the Tater Tots.	Rest.

Best Laid Plans–Meal Planning Emergencies

While planning your meals makes life easy, sometimes the best laid plans go awry! Something suddenly comes up and you can't make it to the store when you planned, or you have a dentist appointment that takes longer than expected and you get home too late to cook. That's life! Here is a way to give your family "something better" in a hurry! Always keep things on hand for emergency meals, remembering that prepackaged foods are higher in fat and sodium than your good home cooking. So use them sparingly!

Canned Goods: Canned beans, canned vegetarian hotdogs, canned soups (reduced sodium, vegetarian), canned fruit in natural juices

Dry Goods: Quick-cooking grains, white and sweet potatoes, whole grain pasta

Prepared sauces: Tomato sauce, salsa

Freezer: Whole grain English muffins and tortillas, pita bread for quick pizza, veggie burgers, frozen vegetables, frozen fruit, vegetarian meat substitutes

BREAKFASTS
Boxed cold cereal (look for cereals with more than 3 grams of fiber and less than 5 grams of sugar)
Bagels and soy cream cheese with fruit
Canned fruit in natural juices

SOUPS & SANDWICHES
Minestrone (page 40)
Low sodium canned soups, like Tomato, Vegetarian Vegetable, or Lentil (watch the labels)
Peanut Butter & Jelly Sandwiches
Vegetarian Lunch Meat slices (page 153)

JUNK FOOD
Vegetarian hot dogs
Frozen vegetarian burgers
Frozen French fries
Sloppy joes, Manwich, and vegetarian beef crumbles

MEXICAN
Quesadillas, made with whole grain tortillas, canned fat-free refried beans mixed with salsa, and whatever veggies you may have
Burrito (page 74, variation)

ITALIAN
Spaghetti with canned sauce (watch the labels for fat and sugar)
Chicken Parmesan (page 66, variation)

INTERNATIONAL
Quick brown rice
Frozen stir-fry vegetables

Glossary

Aluminum-free baking powder: a baking powder that is free from aluminum, which has been proven to cause health problems. We use either the Featherweight or Rumford brands.

Beef style seasoning: a popular all-purpose seasoning used in vegetarian cooking to give a "beefy" type flavor. We use Vegetarian Express brand in our recipes. (thevegetarianexpress.com)

Bragg's Liquid Aminos: a non-fermented soy sauce that is lower in sodium and has a lighter taste. (bragg.com)

Bulgur wheat: a type of whole wheat that has been pre-cooked and dried. It is common in a lot of Middle Eastern foods. We use it as a meaty whole grain substitute for hamburger in our Taco Burger (page 78) and Burger Crumbles (page 78, variation).

Cane juice crystals: evaporated cane juice that retains trace minerals and is minimally processed. Use it cup-for-cup for white sugar.

Carob: a great alternative to chocolate, which contains tannin, caffeine, and theobromine. It is sweeter than chocolate, high in protein, and an excellent source of calcium, potassium, and riboflavin. It is available in powder form (like cocoa powder) and candy form (like chocolate chips). We recommend the barley sweetened carob chips, which do not contain partially-hydrogenated oils.

Chicken Style Seasoning: the most popular all-purpose seasoning in the Adventist world. It is great in a lot of recipes, and some people even eat it on popcorn. We have included a recipe for homemade (page 152), but our favorite commercial brand is from The Vegetarian Express. We also use McKay's chicken style seasoning. (Be sure to look for the dairy- and MSG-free brand) (thevegetarianexpress.com)

Chicken substitute: homemade or store-bought soy and wheat products used to replace chicken in your recipes. There are many store-bought options. (lightlife. com, morningstarfams.com, yvesveggie.com, tofurky. com, gardein.com) See substitutions on page 153 for more information.

Cinnamon substitute: cinnamon can irritate the lining of the stomach and cause irritation of the central nervous system, especially in those who have acid reflux or a sensitive system, so we don't use it in our recipes. We choose to use this mixture of cardamom and coriander in its place. (page 152) It does not taste the same as cinnamon, but it has a wonderful flavor.

Flax seeds: a small brown seed slightly larger than a sesame seed. Its nutrients (omega-3 fatty acids, calcium, iron, niacin, and vitamin E) are most easily absorbed when ground. When mixed with water, they become viscous, adding moisture and binding qualities to your baked goods without the cholesterol. Once flax seed is ground, store it in the freezer to keep it from going rancid.

Gluten flour: also known as vital wheat gluten. It is a part of the wheat kernel that is almost entirely protein. Do not confuse this with "high-gluten flour."

Natural peanut butter: simple and pure, the only ingredients are peanuts and sometimes salt. Because there is no partially hydrogenated oil in natural peanut butter, the oils separate and should be stirred in before use. Store it in the refrigerator after you stir it to keep it from separating again.

Nondairy milks: there are many good options, including soy, rice, almond, oat, and hemp milks. Most are fortified with calcium, vitamin D, and vitamin B12, and some contain sweeteners and flavorings such as vanilla, chocolate, and carob. Taste and richness varies from brand to brand, so keep trying different options until you find one you love.

Non-hydrogenated margarine: a great substitute that can be used like butter in baking and cooking, without the dairy or trans-fats. There are many brands available. Earth Balance and Smart Balance Light are the brands that we use most often.

Nondairy cheese: a substitute for dairy cheese. It comes in several varieties, such as slices, shreds, and blocks. It also comes in many flavors such as cheddar, American, pepper-jack, and parmesan. Our favorite brand is made by Galaxy Nutritional Foods. (galaxyfoods.com)

Nutritional yeast flakes: they are very high in B-vitamins, including B-12, which is a very important vitamin for those who don't eat meat or dairy. It has a unique cheesy type flavor that we use in a lot of recipes.

Pickles or pickle relish: I love to use pickles cured in lemon juice instead of the traditional pickles cured in vinegar, because vinegar can cause some stomach and digestion problems. Besides, the taste is 100% better and the lemon juice helps you to absorb more vitamins. You can find them at the health food store. Our favorite brand is Pa's brand. (pasfoods.com)

Raw cashews: they're just that not roasted or salted. They impart a nice creamy texture to sauces when blended until smooth. They are a great source of protein and antioxidants.

Roma: an instant coffee made from grains, so it is naturally caffeine-free. It is great as a hot drink, but we also like to use it in desserts that use carob to give it a richer, more "chocolaty" flavor. (morningstarfarms.com)

Seitan: also called "wheat meat" or sometimes "gluten," it's a meat substitute made from wheat. It has a great texture and flavor for those who are trying to add something better to their diet. Try our recipe for Gluten Steaks on page 48.

Soy curls: a meat substitute produced by Butler made from the whole soy bean that has been lightly textured. It comes dry and requires "re-hydration" and quite a lot of seasoning. Try our recipe for Prepared Soy Curls on page 150. (butlerfoods.com)

Soy creamer: a dairy-free creamer made by Silk that can be used to replace dairy creamer and half-and-half in recipes. Stir it into Roma or use it in soups and cream sauces for a rich, creamy texture. It comes in Plain, French Vanilla, and Hazelnut flavors.

Soy cream cheese: a dairy-free cream cheese that has a smooth creamy texture and can be used interchangeably in recipes calling for cream cheese.

We like to use Tofutti Cream Cheese, which is non-hydrogenated. (tofutti.com)

Soy mayonnaise: a mayonnaise made without eggs, so it is naturally cholesterol-free. Our favorite brand is Vegenaise for its rich taste and creamy texture. (followyourheart.com) Other options are Nayonaise and Aioli (page 130).

Soy sour cream: a sour cream substitute made from soy. Tofutti "Better than Sour Cream" is our favorite commercial brand. It contains no hydrogenated oils, cholesterol, or dairy. (tofutti.com)

Soy yogurt: a nondairy, soy-based yogurt that replaces dairy yogurt. It comes in many flavors and can be used in recipes for baking, topping a fruit salad, or just eating plain! Be sure to check the ingredients, because some soy yogurts contain dairy. Our favorite brands are Silk and Stonyfield Farm.

Sucanat: a combination of the words "sugar cane natural." Simply, it's cane juice that has been rehydrated, and it has a molasses-like flavor similar to brown sugar. However, it is grainier than brown sugar, so it may not be suitable for every recipe where brown sugar is used.

Tofu: the "curd" made from soy milk, much like cottage cheese, which is made from cow's milk. Tofu comes in two major forms. The water-packed variety requires refrigeration and has a shelf life of about 1 month. This type can be used as a meat, egg, or even cheese substitute. The silken variety is shelf stable for up to 6 months and is very smooth. It is best used in creams and sauces that are blended.

Whole wheat flour: a flour made from hard winter wheat berries with a high gluten content, which makes it perfect for bread. It is made from the entire wheat berry, unlike white or unbleached flour, so it retains all of the vitamins and nutrients found in wheat.

Whole wheat pastry flour: a flour made from soft spring wheat berries with a low gluten content, which makes in better for cakes and cookies. We like to use white whole wheat flour if we can find it, because it is made from the entire wheat berry and is full of vital nutrients. It is lighter in color and makes our cookies and cakes come out lighter and fluffier.

Resources

Contact us and get great resources like:

Menu planning worksheets

Weekly menus

Grocery lists, Etc.

givethemsomethingbetter.blogspot.com

www.sanarelife.com

Where to get the products?

We listed websites in the glossary for most of the products we use. This is the name of a great food co-op where you can get great foods at lower prices.

Country Life Natural Foods (food co-op)

641 52nd St.

Pullman, MI 49450

(800) 456-7694

www.clnf.org

Seasonings:

The Vegetarian Express

www.thevegetarianexpress.com

How do I learn more about Adventists health program?

www.lifestylematters.com

www.chiphealth.com

www.newstart.com

www.ucheepines.org

www.wildwoodlsc.org

www.bhhec.com

How do I learn more about the Sabbath?

www.sabbathtruth.com

How do I learn more about the Bible?

www.glowonline.org

www.amazingfacts.org

www.bibleuniverse.org

www.adventistanswers.org

How do I learn more about Adventists?

www.adventist.org

www.nadeducation.org/who

Where can I watch streaming video with cooking programs and bible studies?

www.3abn.org

www.amazingfacts.tv

Where do I learn more about Blue Zones?

www.bluezones.com

The Blue Zones: Lessons for Living Longer from the People Who've Lived the Longest by Dan Buettner

Index

index

index